BACK TO BACK'S LITTLE BLACK
PAPERBACK BOOK

D1355163

BACK TO BACK'S

LITTLE BLACK PAPER-BACK BOOK

Fraser Grace

KINGSWAY PUBLICATIONS
EASTBOURNE

ISBN 0 86065 384 6

Biblical quotations are from the Good News Bible,
© American Bible Society 1976.

Cover design and text illustrations: Dan Donovan

Printed in Great Britain for
KINGSWAY PUBLICATIONS LTD
Lottbridge Drove, Eastbourne, E. Sussex BN23 6NT by
Cox & Wyman Ltd, Reading.
Typeset by Nuprint Services Ltd, Harpenden, Herts.

Contents

BACK TO BACK

Performing Licence

The sketches in this book are Copyright Back to Back Theatre Co., but you can perform them as many times as you like, where you like, for as long as you like, to whom you like, providing you first get hold of a licence. This licence costs £5, covers all the sketches in this book, and guarantees your right to perform the sketches just so long as you are an amateur group or actor, or a group performing to a non-paying audience. (Fully professional groups must make a separate enquiry.)

You can get a licence by sending the fee, together with your name and address (or the name and address of your group) to:

> Back to Back Theatre Co (Sketches)
> 40 Carlyle Road
> Egbaston
> Birmingham
> B16 9BJ

All the money received will go towards keeping us on the road, and writing more sketches.

Back to Back

Back to Back Theatre Co. was formed in the summer of 1981, since when they have been performing in schools, colleges and universities, and as part of town-wide missions around the country. In addition to week-long mission engagements, the company have also appeared at many of the Christian festivals which take place throughout the year including Greenbelt, Spring Harvest, and Royal Week, and also other Arts festivals such as MayFest (Glasgow), Warrington Arts Festival, and The Edinburgh Festival Fringe.

The present members of the company are Ray Snell, Hazel Brunt and Fraser and Sue Grace. They live in Birmingham, have no children and are too tired for any hobbies.

Kreddits

Many thanks for this book must go to all the people around the country who have supported us in our ministry, either through praying and giving, by living with us, or by agreeing to work with us. For your generosity (in all cases) we are really grateful.

I would also like to give special thanks to my wife Sue, to Ray and to Hazel who together make up the other nine-tenths of Back to Back, and also to our numerous parents and in-laws.

Intro

For some of you this book needs no introduction. You've bought or more likely borrowed it because you've already seen Back to Back in one of the hundreds of performances they've given in schools since their formation in the summer of 1981. If you haven't seen them you were probably playing truant.

Another explanation may be that you were born too late, which is unlikely, or too early, in which case I must apologize; this book is not really aimed at you. I hope, though, that you may still find it useful.

The people this book *is* aimed at are the kind of kids who have already skipped this section in order to get their grubby little hands on the sketches at the back. To you this book is dedicated, in the hope that your energies may be put to good use and your hearts fired with enthusiasm for sharing the Good News. But before you read it—please wash your hands. Someone else may want to borrow it after you.

PART ONE

of
Back to Back's
Little Black
Paperback
Book

Chapter 1

Me and my mates

Forming and Running a Drama Group

Two blokes are leaning on a wall with their backs to us. They are gazing out over acres of wasteland. In the far distance a yellow JCB is lifting another clawful of rubble from one heap and putting it down on another.

'Well,' says the big bloke, taking a deep breath, 'I suppose we *could* form a drama group....'

He breathes out.

Despite the JCB's efforts, the heaps of rubble are still about the same size. Nearby, the wind catches a crisp bag and the two men watch as it scrabbles through the weeds and comes to a stop against an oil drum.

'Yer mean,' begins the thin one, staring intently at the now-static crisp bag. 'Yer mean—perform sketches and that? For charity?'

'Or money,' says the other, shifting his weight. 'On the other hand,' he continues, 'I suppose we *could* do it for reasons of political motivation. To make the point, like.'

'Oh,' says the thin one, thoughtfully. 'I think I'd rather make the money.'

'...or for entertainment of course. I mean, everyone likes a laugh, don't they.'

'I suppose so,' says his mate.

The JCB chugs impatiently and squeezes another cloud of smoke from its latest clawful.

'There. I knew it!' exclaims the thin bloke. 'It's going from right to left. The *left* heap's gettin' bigger....'

'Nah,' says the other, uncertainly, 'I'll stick by what I said.'

'Fine by me,' returns the thin one, and wraps it in a sly smile.

'Of course, we *could* do drama—yer know, to help us, like,' says the big bloke.

A pause.

'Help us what?'

'Well—yer know....'

'No—what?'

'Well, sort of...I mean it might er....'

'Yeah?'

'You know....'

'What?!'

'Well...it might...*help* us, yer know—to talk about things what we find difficult to talk about....'

'Oh I see,' says the thin one. 'Yer mean, use drama

14

primarily as a means of expression rather than as communication?'

'Yeah—that's it,' says the big one.

'Nah—don't fancy that much. I'd rather say somethin' funny—and get the money.'

'Yer get more if yer bein' funny *and* sayin' somethin' ...' warns the big bloke.

The heap of rubble on the right hand side has finally begun to get bigger. The JCB, sensing victory, begins to speed up, squeezing every last drop from the debris before dropping it and returning for more. The mountain on the left has suddenly become a mole hill.

'Rats!' says the thin man, and begins to dig into his pocket. A coin passes from the thin bloke to the big bloke.

'Ta.'

'Goin' back to this drama group thing,' says the thin one, moving off down the road. 'Who'll be in it?'

'Ah,' says the big bloke, catching him up. 'Now yer talkin'....'

That's what this book is talking about too—drama! In this chapter we're going to look at how a drama group gets together and, especially, how it should keep going. So—if you're interested, why not buy the book and read it at home?

Thank you.

Where was I? Oh yeah—forming and running a drama group. Well, for a start, people *do* drama for all sorts of reasons, like the big bloke said.... Sue and Ray, the founder members of Back to Back (which, I hasten to add, was not started in the way described above) began 'doing drama' at university. They both got kind of sucked into it because the Christian Union there

15

had a drama group which was doing something different. And it wasn't only different. The people in the group obviously thought that what they were doing was important too. The idea was to go out to different halls of residence, bars, or any other place where the students hung out, and tell them about Jesus by performing sketches. Later on the group, called Travelling Players, started branching out into local schools and shopping precincts doing the same sort of stuff, for the same sort of reasons, and getting a bit of a reputation for itself. Apart from being very committed to evangelism—that is, telling other people about Jesus so that they can become his disciples too—the group also became a really good place for fellowship: people were working and praying together and caring for one another in a way that most of the members had never known before. So I suppose it's not *that* surprising that what happened *did* happen.

Over a period of a few months, Sue and Ray began to feel that God was speaking quite directly to them saying that they should carry on doing this sort of thing when they left college, and that it would be their job.

What?! Yes, God was speaking to students. Not in any blinding flashes though—in fact in some ways it was pretty ordinary.

It all started when, together with the rest of the group, Sue and Ray began to see how well drama worked in schools. Even though the sketches they were doing at the time weren't really suitable for school kids, they could still be used to grab people's attention, and people were hearing about Jesus. Unfortunately, because students are supposed to do some work as well, there wasn't much time left to spend in school, and that was when the idea landed. Wouldn't it be good if, instead of having to study or try and get a job, you could do drama full time? That way you could do the job properly.

Once they discovered that they were both thinking the same thing, Sue and Ray decided to pray about it. If it really was an idea which God had given them, then he wouldn't mind if he was asked to confirm it. So that's what they asked God to do, and as they met to pray each week, bits from the Bible began to crop up again and again, saying that they shouldn't be afraid and that God was going to provide everything they needed: it was his idea.

On top of this, Ray and Sue also asked other people's advice and most agreed that it was a good idea and felt that God was speaking. Finally, Sue and Ray's own feelings began to change; worries about how they would write material, where they would live and how they could ever find enough money to survive began to be replaced by a trust in the promises that God had so generously given them and a determination to see it through.

Four years later, they are still seeing it through. And, more importantly, God has kept all of his promises.

After the first twelve months, it was clear that the group should continue and grow, so Back to Back expanded into a company of four. That meant the addition of me, Fraser (another ex-Travelling Player) and Hazel, who gave up the glory of working in an off-licence in Cumbria for the delights of Birmingham! So God can and does speak to people today.

Why the name? We chose Back to Back as a name because lots of the Bible images that God used to speak to Sue and Ray were about building: our heroes felt that God wanted to use them to build 'spiritual homes' for people who didn't know God. If you like, people who have left God out of their lives, have left their proper 'home' and have become 'spiritually homeless'. As well as that, Sue and Ray felt that God wanted them to stay in Birmingham and work from there, so we wanted a name which tied together buildings and cities. Back to Back is the name given to the old type of houses (like those in *Coronation Street*) which were built in Birmingham and other cities, and were later knocked down to make way for office blocks and multi-storey car parks. Now, people used to say that Back to Back houses were too small and over-crowded, but if you came to Birmingham and walked down the main road just around the corner from our house, you'd see block after block of the kind of offices which were built in their place. All the blocks have thousands and thousands of square feet of office space and loads of them are completely empty and have been ever since they were built.

Isn't that a picture of what we allow the devil to do when we're continually disobedient to God? He tears down the 'home' with God that we were intended to have, and puts in its place something hugely empty and useless. God wants to rebuild proper 'homes' for people, and he's using us and many others to do it.

Anyway, that's how we got started, a bit about why we started and also how we got our name.

What about you? Maybe your group, if you're in one, started in a different way: just you and a few mates getting together to do a sketch for the vicar at church. Or perhaps you felt that drama would be a more interesting way to teach the kids in Sunday School. You might even have got into drama through doing it at school or college, and would like to know how to go about using it for God. Our first suggestion to you is to consider getting some of the other books we mention, and which are listed under 'More to Read' at the back of this book. That's not a cop-out—just an admission that we can't tell you everything. In fact, we can only really tell you about using drama for evangelism—as the subtitle suggests—because that's about all we've done. We can't tell you much about musical drama, dance or mime either, but what we can do, at least in this chapter and the one which follows, is put down some principles that any Christians ought to think about and, hopefully, act on (sorry) when forming and running a drama group. So here goes.

Forming a drama group
Members

I suppose the first thing to ask—as the thin bloke eventually did—is: 'Who'll be in it?' This is a bit of a tricky one really, because if you're starting from scratch the people in the group will have to decide what sort of group they want it to be. On the other hand, it's also true that people will probably want to know what sort of group they are being asked to join!

To sort this one out, it's best to pray that God will provide the people he wants to use for this project, and then call a meeting. Anyone who is interested in joining a drama group can come. Then, when it has been decided how the group will operate, people can decide whether or not they want to be involved.

Types of group

There are really only two types of group I can think of. Firstly, there is the kind of *ad hoc* or occasional group which often exists in a church, youth group or Christian Union. It consists of a number of people who are brought together now and again to do a sketch when the need or opportunity arises. This might only be a few times a year. If your group is like this, its size will probably vary quite a lot from time to time, and the particular people in it may also differ according to who's available. A group like this might not need to think very carefully about these first three chapters, although if you do read them it may help you to see how your group could develop.

A second type of group is the kind which is formed in order to function as a drama group on a more long-term basis, as our group at university did. The main difference between this and the last sort is the level of commitment needed. This kind of group is also more likely to develop an identity of its own, a name which it sticks to, and will begin to look for and make opportunities to perform. It should also have a pretty good idea as to why it exists—which brings us to the next point.

Aims

Any group which comes into the second category above, or anyone who is thinking about starting a group like that, should take time to decide what the aims of the group are to be.

Here are some guidelines to help you:

1. The first guideline is that as Christians our chief aim must always be to please God. So, if you're just interested in drama because you fancy being a star (or because you fancy someone else in the group)—forget it.

Being committed to a drama group which really

wants to serve God means hard work, even though it will be enjoyable too. So start off with the intention purely of pleasing yourself and you will not only be disappointed, you will also be without a hope of pleasing God.

2. Although most Christians would approve of the first guideline, a lot of the drama groups I've come across don't seem to have much idea when it comes to specific aims. Yet, as the big bloke realized, drama can be used for loads of different things. If your group is a bit vague on the subject, then the second guideline must be to pray together, perhaps with a sympathetic minister or youth leader. Ask God to show you where you as a group should concentrate your efforts. Will it be in producing sketches for church services, Sunday School or youth fellowship, in other words, teaching and encouraging Christians? If so, ask your minister to let you know the themes or passages he will be speaking on well in advance (if he is that organized!), or check the themes yourself if, for instance, your Sunday School works to a set plan.

If you feel that communicating the gospel to non-Christians is what you are chiefly called to, then begin to think about the places where, if you like, your church brushes shoulders with 'the world': an open youth club, uniformed organizations like the Boys' and Girls' Brigade or Scouting groups. Find out about them, and talk to the leaders. Would they be willing to let you perform one night? If your group is based in a school or college Christian Union, then make one of your meetings an open one where the members can bring their friends to see a performance. You might even decide to set up a special event, say on a Friday night at church, maybe inviting other people such as musicians or your minister to be involved as well.

The important things to remember are:
1. To plan well in advance.
2. To keep those in authority over you in touch with what you are doing.
3. To be clear as to what your aims as a group are.

You will become more certain of those aims as you wait on God. Turn back a few pages and re-read the account of how God spoke to Sue and Ray. What ways did he use? Those are some of the ways you can expect to hear answers.

Lastly, I want to emphasize that this doesn't mean you will necessarily be absolutely 100% sure of your aims before you ever set foot on stage. But, you will have committed the whole thing to God and be in a state of openness to him. And you will have started to discover what God's aims are for you as a group. When you've begun to do that, you will need to turn your attention to the practical matters of keeping it going.

Running a drama group

Organization

The first step here, if you haven't done it already, is to organize a weekly rehearsal time and place—probably an evening or sometime over the weekend when everyone can get together to talk, pray, study the Bible and rehearse. This will be the time when most of the 'head work' will get done. You may also need to set up extra time to rehearse, but that can be done as and when you need it.

Now is a good time to think about a name too, and you may also need to find a leader.

Leadership

The leader's main responsibility is to make sure things get done: where and at what time is the next performance? Do we need extra rehearsal time to get this sketch up to scratch? Has somebody checked that all the props are in order? Who's going to do the publicity? Can we have a coffee break?

The leader should also take a large part of the responsibility for the spiritual well-being of the group. Does everybody feel happy about the way things are going? Has someone been asked to lead the prayer time next week, or to organize a short Bible study? Is anyone feeling really fed up and in need of some encouragement? Who is going to *make* the coffee?

Over a period of time, you will probably find that different people in the group end up 'leading' in different areas. For instance, you may discover that two people are particularly good at writing, so they will tend to 'lead' the efforts around that area. Others might be good at directing, making props or doing publicity—fine, the lads can make the coffee!

Whatever the case, a leader can only lead if everyone else agrees to let them, by submitting to his or her judgement. St Paul tells us to do this anyway out of reverence for Christ (Eph 5), so the practice will do us good. Another thing to remember is that leaders are only leaders in the biblical sense if they see themselves as a servant to the rest of the group and act accordingly. In fact, the attitude in the group as a whole should be that you are there to serve each other in order to fulfil your aims and to build one another up. The group in turn should think of itself as a servant to the rest of the church and those outside it.

Physical preparation

As well as talking, praying, thinking and studying, now is a good time to begin training yourselves physically and mentally for the task of acting.

Physical fitness and dramatic skills can be improved in a number of ways, most obviously by doing exercises. There are plenty of cassettes around to help you do this, including some by Christians, and it's certainly one of the most popular methods at the moment. An even more interesting way, though, is by playing games.

First of all—as all the best books say—wear loose-fitting clothing and casual footwear or bare feet. (If you can't bear to leave the house with baggy trousers on, stuff them in a bag and change out of your jeans when you get there.) OK you're looking good. Now to begin with you'll need to warm up. All of us can think of games we used to play in the playground at Junior School which involve running about and generally exhausting yourself. Most of them use some sort of 'tag' where one person chases all the others until he or she catches one or all of them. Then someone else takes over. Dobby Scarecrow (also known as Stick-in-the-Mud) is a good one, but use any you can think of. Then, loosened up, you're ready to move on to 'skill' games and exercises.

Development of drama skills

Some of the most useful skills for drama are things like concentration, physical co-ordination, sense of rhythm, balance, trust, team work, voice control and projection and imagination. These skills, and exercises to help you develop them, are very well covered in Clive Barker's book *Theatre Games* and more simply in the Bible Society's book *Using the Bible in Drama*, coedited by Steve and Janet Stickley of Footprints Theatre Co. Others can be found in the numerous books dealing with movement and dance (although these will tend towards straight exercises). Be willing to glean ideas from these books—and also any workshops you have the chance to attend—and try them out together. Some exercises are harder than others, and you may feel a bit vulnerable when trying to do them in front of the rest of the group. Be aware of this when watching and be ready to encourage each other rather than going in for one-upmanship. The idea is to help each other to learn and discover abilities which will make your acting crisper and seemingly effortless, so that people will hear what God is saying through your drama rather than your creaking bones.

Lastly, always try to leave time at the end of a session to fix a date for the next rehearsal. Then thank God for the things you've been able to learn and achieve. Thank him, too, for each other and commit all your work and relationships to him. Be willing as well to encourage others in their walk with God generally, and to share your experiences with them— remember there's more to life than drama, and whatever use your drama is put to, God wants to speak through your unity and love for one another, as much as through your sketches.

So, the group is formed, your aims are gelling, your prayers are rising and your muscles are aching—but what are you going to say?

Chapter 2

Learning to be a sieve-head

Listening to God and Finding Material

If you've started thinking, talking and praying through your aims as a group, then you've already taken the first step towards becoming a first-rate sieve-head! Let me explain.

When I was still knee-high to a grasshopper, I was trundled along to Sunday School like loads of other kids. Once a month we were allowed into the chapel for the Family Service. On these and other occasions—like the annual Sunday School Anniversary—I would sit and look at the rows and rows of old ladies at the back of the chapel. All of them had very severe faces, and very big hats. I used to wonder why, when they were singing hymns that said they were really glad about God, and saying 'Amen' to prayers that were thanking God for everything he'd done for them, they still looked so miserable. I gave this a lot of thought and eventually I cracked it! It was the hats!

This is how it worked: years ago, God had in some way spoken to each of these ladies, and they had all accepted Jesus into their lives. Since then, they'd all been singing and talking away to God, but their hats were like steel helmets which stopped God's Spirit getting through. So all they had was memories, and in the meantime they got more and more empty—all because of the hats! I made up my mind that I would never wear a hat in church—which was just as well, since the men had to take theirs off anyway. In fact, it wasn't until a few years later I discovered that, although you wouldn't always know it from their faces, some of these ladies really loved God. I also noticed that some of the men looked even more miserable, which meant that there had to be a bit more to it than just your choice of headgear—maybe even more than your choice of wife!

Nonetheless, lots of people are very good at talking to God—in fact so good that God can hardly get a word in edgeways—but aren't prepared to listen. They've got their 'hats' firmly in place. Now, I know being called a 'sieve-head' doesn't sound too flattering but at least if you had a sieve on your head, there'd be a few holes for God's Spirit to get through, wouldn't there?

Learning to be a sieve-head is all about training yourself to be aware of what God is saying, and allowing his Spirit to mould your thinking, so that more and more you will have 'the mind of Christ'. This is

especially important when you're involved in something like drama which demands lots of enthusiasm
and energy and is such good fun. There's every temp-
tation to push on ahead and maybe perform things
because they're funny or easy but actually don't really
speak so much about God as about the fact that you're
having a great time. So you've got to use your judgement, and that's only reliable when you've submitted
it to God.

For example, when you get to the stage of looking
for material to perform, say for a church service, you
want something that is relevant to the theme of the
service (if it has a strong one) and which says what
God wants to say about it in a fresh way to the sort of
people who will be watching and listening. It's very
easy for us to point our finger at people and say what
we think, but God's words are good and have a power
far beyond that which a live performance automatically gives. So you will need to discuss your choice of
material as a group, committing it to God and asking
him to use it for his glory.

Where do we look for material?

One place to look, and perhaps the easiest place to
find it, is a book like this one. All you have to do is buy
the book, pay for a licence, perform all the sketches
you think you can do, and then look around for another book of sketches.

This has some advantages, as well as some disadvantages.

Advantages

One of the most obvious advantages is that published

material is generally written to a high standard by professional writers or companies. Perhaps, as in this book, the sketches will be accompanied by hints to tell you how best to rehearse and perform them. Other attractions are that you've possibly seen the company in question performing these very sketches. In that case, you'll have a good idea of how they 'should be done'. Also, if you've enjoyed seeing the sketches and thought they were good, then there's every reason to expect other people will too. Anyway, 'There's no one in our group who can write sketches.'

All these considerations combine to make a persuasive argument in favour of using 'tried and tested' sketches written by other people. And it's certainly true that, if you're just starting out, rehearsing and performing a script that you know is reliable can be a real help. For a start, you get a feel of how to structure a sketch yourself. It also helps you to be more confident as an actor or actress because providing you pour in plenty of energy, work well as a group and deliver your lines well (and providing that the audience is reasonably relaxed and friendly) you will get a good response. That, as all actors know, is important and encouraging.

Given all these advantages, it's no wonder that published material is so much in demand, but I'd like to suggest that there are also several disadvantages in always using other people's sketches.

Disadvantages

Firstly, and most obviously, there is a very limited amount of published material available. People often come up to us and say that they've got bored with their drama group because they've run out of sketches to do. Very few of these people have ever thought or tried to write their own sketches. That's the second disadvantage. Published scripts can be very useful to learn from—providing a wide enough selection is used to avoid getting into a stylistic rut, but they can easily prevent a group ever trying to create their own sketches. After all, if you can skip the whole problem of having to force yourself to pray for ideas and trying to turn those ideas into sketches—why bother? Stress isn't good for you! Well of course you might bother for the practical reason mentioned above—because you've run out of published sketches to perform. But there are also other reasons.

Writing your own sketches

Let's go back a bit and put our sieves on. We need to hear from God, so get your Bible out and look up Exodus 4:1–10. Now Moses was not having a good day—he's in the blue corner. God, who starts getting a bit angry later on, is in the red corner. Moses versus God, to see who's the greatest. Round one, Ding-Ding, and they're away.... The problem was that Moses was not very good with his mouth. That doesn't mean he swore a lot, he just wasn't very good at talking.

Some people, like me, are not very good with their hands. No matter how hard I try, I just can't saw in a straight line. If you came to our house, and looked very closely at all the woodwork, you'd see that every single edge is absolutely straight. That's because I let Ray do it all. Or map reading—I'm useless! So when we're travelling around, Sue does all the navigating.

Moses was useless with his mouth, and God had asked him to be his No. 1 spokesman.

'Me?' yelped Moses. 'But I get all me wrongs the word way round! And anyway, what will I say?'

'Don't worry about that,' says God. 'I made your mouth, I'll teach you what to say.'

'No—I send you'd better think someone else...' says Moses.

Moses kept on saying no to God because he was too scared, and didn't trust God to give him the right words. In the end, God had to send Moses' brother Aaron to do the talking, but he still told Moses what to say. That way Moses had to tell Aaron, and Aaron had to tell everyone else, which was all much more complicated than it needed to be, even if it did create a job for Aaron. I suppose you could say that on this occasion, God won on a technical knockout.

Now look carefully at the way God planned things. He called Moses to do a job and wanted to give him the things he needed in order to do it. In this case that meant all sorts of miraculous signs, plus the words to say and the ability to say them clearly. (The problem only arose because Moses didn't want to take the risk.) And generally when God calls anyone to do anything for him, he promises to help them. In fact, he insists that they let him do the job through them. So if God wants to use your drama group to speak to other people, won't he want to help by telling you what to say and helping you to say it?

Take another example. If a preacher stood up in your church and read someone else's sermon word for word, maybe in someone else's accent, you would probably think it was a bit weird. OK, some of it might be really good and helpful, but after a while

you'd probably begin to think it was a bit strange.
After all, if the preacher felt that God had asked him to
preach, then why not preach a sermon of his own?
Admittedly, he might have learnt something from
another preacher, but wouldn't it be better if he could
put it into his own words? And if God had called him
to preach, then surely he would have given him
experiences of his own to draw on which would add to
the message. Or even a slightly different angle on the
passage in question. And what about a few better
jokes—they wouldn't go amiss either!

Now apply that sort of thinking to your drama
group. God has put you together to do a job. He could
have chosen just about anyone to serve him in this
way at this time, but he chose you. You've all got
different personalities, interests and slightly different
ways of thinking, and it's through *this* combination
that God has chosen to express just some of the ideas
and lessons he wants to give to the rest of the people in
your patch. Because of that it's bound to come out a bit
different through you than through any other group.
You may well be saying the same sort of things, but
you will naturally express them in a slightly different
way which is special to you. Because it is special to
you, it may be a bit more meaningful to those who are
going to hear and see it.

Go for it!

God is ready to help you if you will ask him. The very
act of asking and receiving will strengthen your faith,
help you know more about God and know him better
as a person. It will also help draw the members of your
group closer to each other because you've risked your-

selves together, trusted God together, maybe struggled with failure together and, eventually, created something together. God is a creator, you've become a bit more like him. And, now that you've become a load of sieve-heads and been willing to risk it and step out in faith, God will be all the more able to touch people through you. Your drama and your ministry as a group have begun to develop a 'prophetic' aspect because you are speaking out of what God has given you to say.

Of course, I don't mean by all this that once you've prayed about it sketches will flow from your biro like toothpaste from a tube, or that your sketches will automatically be brilliant. I don't recommend either that you put on your publicity: 'All sketches written by the Holy Spirit, copyright Heaven 1985,' or whatever.

I could show you drawers full of absolute junk that we've written! Sometimes we've performed the sketches once or twice and found that they didn't really work. Some of these we've thrown away, others have been rewritten several times and have eventually 'come good'. Others have been fine from the start. All of them have come about through a mixture of inspiration and perspiration, and often you don't realize that there is any inspiration in there until you've finished it, and rehearsals have begun. The thing is, regardless of how good or bad they are, they are your sketches. As you take the risk of trusting God more, creating more of your own sketches and relying on other people's material less and less, your sketches will get better and better. Remember, we're not saying don't ever use published material, but what we are saying is use it, learn from it, and then move on....

That's the way we'd like you to use the sketches in this book, and later on I'll be giving you some ideas on how to go about actually creating your own. But, first, who are you going to perform to? In the next chapter I'll be assuming, for reasons mentioned in chapter one, that your group wants to use drama mainly for evangelism. But who are you going to evangelize, and how will that affect what sort of material you will need to come up with?

Chapter 3

Oy, Fishface – Knoworramean?

Choosing, Knowing and Communicating with Your Audience

'As Jesus walked along the shore of Lake Galilee, he saw two brothers who were fishermen, Simon (called Peter) and his brother Andrew, catching fish in the lake with a net. Jesus said to them, "Come with me, and I will teach you to catch men"' (Mt 4:18–19).

Imagine for a minute that instead of talking to fishermen, Jesus had said those words to a woman he met later on—the woman of Samaria, as she is known. Do you know the story? It's in John 4. Jesus was sitting by the well when a woman came to fetch water, and because he was thirsty Jesus asked her for a drink. That was pretty amazing for a start, because Jews like

Jesus weren't supposed to have anything to do with Samaritans, least of all Samaritan women. Anyway, they got talking. After a while, Jesus—who could see right into her life—said:

'Go and call your husband and come back.'

'I haven't got a husband,' she answered.

Imagine if Jesus had replied in the same way that he spoke to Simon and Andrew:

'Come with me, and I will teach you to catch men'!

Somehow I think she might have got the wrong idea. Yet Jesus was calling both the fishermen and the woman to leave their lives of sin and to follow him.

Why did it matter what words he used? The answer is obvious: Jesus was sensitive to people's situations and needs. He used the image of catching to call Simon and Andrew to follow him, because he knew that as fishermen they would know what he was getting at. There was no way they could have understood all that would be involved in following Jesus—how could they? But they understood what catching was all about, knew that men were more valuable than fish, and followed him.

Likewise with the woman of Samaria. In John's account of their meeting, Jesus starts off by talking about water, because that was one of the things her life revolved around. He knew that every day she would have to fetch water from the well. Jesus also knew that despite having lived with six different men, she was still deeply dissatisfied with her life—so catching men was the last thing she needed calling to! Instead, Jesus talked about God's life as being 'living water' that would quench her thirst for ever, and the woman knew she wanted to know more. We're even told that because of her testimony, loads of people from her town believed in Jesus, and many more went to check it out for themselves, and they also became his followers.

Now, admittedly, things weren't always that simple. If you read John's Gospel from beginning to end, you'd see that Jesus almost always used figures of speech when teaching the people around him. This was because he always knew where his life and teaching would lead him—to the cross. He had to be careful to go only at God the Father's pace in getting there, so he said things in an indirect way and left people to work it out. You'll also see that this could be pretty frustrating for the twelve disciples who were particularly close to him—in fact on a number of occasions it all got a bit too much for them:

'We don't know what he's talking about!' they complained.

And eventually when Jesus did 'tell them straight' about God being his Father, and that it was God who had sent him in the first place, the disciples breathed a huge sigh of relief.

'Now you are speaking plainly, without using figures of speech. We know now that you know everything; you do not need someone to ask you questions. This makes us believe that you came from God' (Jn 16:29–30).

But let's leave aside the disciples' frustrations for a minute because there are a couple of important lessons we can learn from Jesus' way of doing things.

Jesus' audience

The first lesson is that Jesus' teaching was delivered to ordinary people and outcasts. These people—who had been rejected by the more 'upright' citizens of the day—were the sort of people that Jesus chose to spend nearly all his time with, and they were also his audience when he spoke. There were exceptions to this of course. For instance, Jesus often tried to teach the Jewish 'faithfuls' in the synagogue, and some believed because of it. The Bible also tells us of several occasions when 'special' individuals like the rich young ruler or Nicodemus the Jewish teacher approached him. There were doubtless many more occasions like these, but notice that these people came and found Jesus—not the other way round. In fact, one of the Pharisees' chief complaints was that Jesus spent all his time with 'sinners', which the Pharisees themselves considered to be in very bad taste:

'Why does your teacher eat with such people?' they asked the disciples (Mt 9:11). And the rest of Matthew is full of references to 'the crowd' containing, alongside honest working men and women, prostitutes, tax gatherers, beggars, thieves and so on. In reply to the Pharisees, Jesus said clearly that these were the very people he had come for and that he came not to judge them, but to bring them salvation. He told them:

'People who are well do not need a doctor, but only those who are sick...I have not come to call respectable people, but outcasts' (Mt 9:12–13).

So it seems that while Jesus willingly accepted all those who believed and took his message to heart, whatever their status, he felt a particular yearning that ordinary working people and in particular the poor, the blind, the sick and all the other social 'parasites' of the day should discover the new life which he brought. It was for that reason they became his chosen audience.

In this chapter I'd like to suggest that if our aim is to

relay the Good News to people who haven't heard it, then we should ask God to take us to the sort of places and the sort of people that Jesus went to. That way his message will be delivered to his chosen audience. As James had to remind all God's people scattered over the whole world, 'God chose the poor people of this world to be rich in faith and to possess the kingdom which he promises to those who love him' (Jas 2:5).

But it's not only *where* and to *whom* we present the Good News that's important, is it? I mean, what about the *way* in which we present it—the language we use?

That's the second lesson we need to learn from Jesus' way of teaching.

It's the way yer tell 'em

Not only was Jesus' way of teaching very entertaining, he also made the message, which God had given him, directly relevant to the crowd. Or, perhaps it's more correct to say, Jesus made the relevance of God's message *apparent to them*. Jesus showed the crowd that this message, which came from God, was for *them*. He did this not only by living his life among them, as we have already seen, but also by the way he taught them. He constantly chose images which had to do with the everyday lives of the crowd—the people who were listening.

So, he talked to the woman of Samaria about water and the fishermen about fishing. Other stories are about kings, servants, shepherds, sheep, light, darkness, parties, bread (and lack of it), grapevines, farmers, seeds, fruit and so on—all things which touched on the lives, or dreams, of ordinary people.

41

Problems

Now Jesus understood what the lives of such people were all about—largely because he was one of them, and that may cause us some problems. After all, most people in most churches are fairly well off, fairly well educated and in fairly good jobs. Many people outside the church aren't: they tend to leave school early with few qualifications. They are therefore more likely to have jobs which involve manual labour—that is, work of a physical rather than mental nature, whether that be skilled, semi-skilled or unskilled. Many will end up with illnesses caused by or related to the kind of work they do—illnesses which are almost unknown among people who have more 'comfortable' and, usually, better paid jobs. Some will even die earlier because of it. Others, of course, will have no job at all and others still will be 'unemployable' because of physical or mental handicap or illness. These people will probably read different newspapers, watch different TV programmes and videos, and eat different meals than most of the kind of people who go to church. In fact, most of them will never have set foot in church, except perhaps when they were christened, or perhaps later when they got married or went to a funeral. Even less will have understood what went on when they did go, and even less than that will have ever heard, or even thought about Jesus dying for them.

Just recently we met a boy in Bradford who had never heard that God loved him and had sent Jesus to die for him, and didn't know he could get to know God for himself. Now, Darren was only ten, but I bet his mum and dad and his older brother had never heard it either. Darren only needed to hear the Good News once, explained in a way which he could begin to understand, and he knew he wanted to be a Christian. And we meet hundreds of people like Darren all over the country. Because their experience of life so far is very different from ours, and because they've never heard the gospel (or if they have, they've not realized it is for people like them), they've got a whole different outlook on life.

This means that if I want to communicate with Jesus' audience, I may have to speak to people with whom I don't have much in common. I have to recognize that this difference is partly the result of my own lifestyle—a lifestyle which could be a lot nearer to Christ's if it wasn't for my own ignorance, reluctance and sometimes disobedience towards God's claims on different parts of my life. So I must be willing to change in some ways. The difference is also of course a result of my education, family and many other things which in normal circumstances I couldn't and shouldn't want to disown. But none of these things should stop me being willing to learn a new language, a new way of thinking in order to communicate God's truth to those who need it most. In fact my faith in Jesus, which should have changed my outlook more than anything else, will make me want to learn that language as well as I can, so that people will realize that Jesus came to save *them*.

It is necessary to learn that new language if I want to use the dramatic gifts God has given me.

The problem with drama

The problem with drama is that lots of people never go to the theatre, at least not before it's taken over by Ladbrokes and turned into a Bingo club. Some people don't go because they can't afford it. An evening out at one of London's West End theatres, or at the local Repertory Theatre, can work out pretty expensive by the time you've got there, bought the tickets, paid for a programme, had a drink during the interval and caught the bus home again. Others don't go because they don't know anyone else who's ever been and it's just not something you think of doing. Still others are put off because they went once, say on a school trip, and they couldn't understand what was going on: 'Why was everyone all dressed up? Why did everyone keep telling us to be quiet? And why didn't that bloke in the tights answer me back when I told him he looked like a Christmas cake?! I thought they were always supposed to be ready with a quick joke. And as for that woman—anyone could see she was at least fifty, and there she was makin' out she was sweet sixteen! Stupid, I reckon. Not to mention borin'....'

It's pretty obvious that that sort of theatre isn't going to mean much to most of the kids at school, for instance, regardless of the fact that the play might have a Christian theme. Let me give you another example, this time from Back to Back's own experience.

In 1982, we performed a play at the Edinburgh Festival Fringe. About four hundred other groups were performing at the same time in halls and theatres all over the city. The play we performed was the first full-length play I'd ever written, and although our audiences weren't massive, they were pretty good by

Edinburgh standards and we got good reviews from the newspapers. On top of that, people who weren't Christians, but who enjoyed seeing plays, enjoyed it and in some cases were made to think quite seriously about God. That was our aim, so we were quite rightly encouraged by the fact that all our praying and hard work had been fruitful. Nonetheless, the play simply would not have worked in school, for instance, because it tested the endurance of all but the keenest theatre-goer. Long periods of the play were spent in total silence, with very little movement. The humour in it was of a pretty intellectual kind—funny if you're 'in the know' but a bit bewildering if not. And, above all, the play at first glance asked more questions than it answered.

Despite all that, we still think the play was a worthwhile project, and we certainly don't regret doing it. But the people we really want to spend our time trying to reach are the people Jesus spent his time with, and to perform that play in an open youth club or an old people's home would be almost impossible. It demands concentration that they are unlikely to have; a knowledge of the work of one particular writer which they probably haven't had the opportunity of studying; and an understanding of what 'conventional' theatre is all about, that is, me performing and you listening. Quietly. Now the message of the play is just as relevant to youth club kids and old people as it is to anyone else, but the structure, form and style of the play would combine to spell out: 'This is not for you.' Accordingly, the performance would result in either a mass walk-out or a riot in the youth club, and very loud snoring in the old people's home.

So what can we do?

1. Style

If God has called us to present the gospel through drama to the people whom Jesus came to save, we need to learn how to get the message over in ways which say: 'Don't switch off—this is for you.' We must develop styles of drama that succeed where the conventional styles fail. In other words, if people aren't very good at concentrating, then we'll have to make our drama loud, fast-moving and sharp. If they like jokes to be big and bold, even slapstick, then I won't make them feel stupid by putting in jokes which are too subtle or obscure for them to get. Or, if they like a good story, I'll try to make up a story that gets over what I want to say, but which at the same time is exciting, funny, and sad (or whatever else they want in it, within reason!).

And we can't assume they know all about the Bible, so if we do use a Bible story, we'll make sure they know who told it first, and we'll also make sure the jokes in it don't rely on people knowing the original.

To do all this we'll need to widen our sources of inspiration, and there are loads of other places beside the theatre and the *Play for Today* slot on TV that use dramatic forms. How about the adverts on TV? They use short, sharp images and humour to get over a message—even if it is only why you should use one kind of washing-up liquid, or drink one kind of beer, rather than another.

What about pantomimes? If you've ever been to one it was probably in a theatre, but it will hardly have been like the conventional plays we've talked about. That's because there's a whole different set of 'con-

ventions' or dramatic rules in operation in a panto-
mime. The idea here is for the audience to make as
much noise as possible, especially when the monster
is about to attack the hero. Apart from yelling 'it's
behind yer' the audience is also treated to songs,
comedy and romance. Someone fills us in on the story
so far, we see bits of the story actually acted out and so
on. There's lots of variety and always something going
on to hold our interest—that might give us an idea of
how to put together a good programme.

What about those story videos, or that new game
that's just come out, or the competitions in the paper?
All these are kinds of entertainment, most are
'dramatic' in some way and nearly all have some kind
of message—however vague and inadequate com-
pared with ours. And the characters—what about
those? *Coronation Street* must be the most popular
British TV programme of all time—it uses lots of
scenery, make-up and some really good actors and
actresses, so there's probably no way we could do the
same sort of thing. But we could make references to it,
and even have characters that are similar. A character
like Hilda Ogden, for instance, is instantly recognizable to most adults and crops up in lots of other
places besides *Coronation Street*. The old music hall
presentations were littered with people like Hilda—
the cleaner/gossip would come on, tell a few jokes,
sing a sad song about how hard her work was (or
sometimes a rude song) and maybe introduce the next
act. She's there again in the Cinderella panto, this
time played by a man and thinly disguised as Widow
Twanky or an Ugly Sister. She's even in at least one of
the sketches in this book! (I'll leave you to discover
where.)

All these different dramatic forms, their characters, languages and styles are there for us to learn from. And, thankfully, we are not completely alone in the task: many contemporary theatre companies, touring and community groups, are also struggling to learn from these different, 'popular' dramatic forms in order to reach the same audience. Needless to say, most of these companies are not Christian-based, but many of them have a philosophy based on political ideals of one kind or another and so have a particular message which they want to communicate. Because we know that the Holy Spirit can achieve through our drama far more than the power of a live performance alone can achieve, that is no reason to ignore the lessons such groups have had to learn. For example, John McGrath, writing from a socialist viewpoint writes in his book *A Good Night Out*:

> To create a kind of theatre that tells the story from a different perspective, in a language that a different group of people understand, i.e. to create a working class form of theatre appropriate to the twentieth century, we have to look at the language of working class entertainment, at least to see what kind of language it is.

The book goes on to describe some of the forms which that language takes, as I have tried to do, and also very usefully describes some of the attempts which he and his company (7:84 Theatre Company) have made in adopting and adapting that language to their particular purpose. Now, as Mr McGrath clearly states, and as we must doubly be aware of, that doesn't mean that we uncritically accept as useful every form or characterization we see used: some may be totally inappropriate and, to our eyes, offensive to the gospel. And obviously 'the story' to which Mr McGrath himself refers will not be the one which is central to our message. But isn't what he describes at least part of what we as Christians must do (and of course, some have begun to do) in order to use our dramatic skills to reach that 'different group of people' with the Good News of Jesus Christ?

2. Content

Our wish to choose and communicate with Jesus' audience will also affect the content as well as the style and venues of our drama. We want to be uncompromising in our presentation of the gospel, but it has got to make sense to the people who will watch and hear our performances. We must get to know our audience as Jesus did. You can begin by finding out what questions your friends have got about God, or what their biggest problem with God is.

Try to think things out together as a group: what is it that keeps people from accepting God into their lives? Ignorance? Be direct though sensitive in your sketches and tell them what Jesus said and did. Is it pride? What does the Bible say about pride? How about money and their attachment to it? What did Jesus say about that? Do they think it's wet to be a Christian? What was Jesus really like? What does Jesus demand of us if we want to follow him? Try to answer questions that people are asking, and if they're not asking any, try to think why. Is it because their lives are so miserable that they can't believe anyone loves them? Tell them someone does, and let them ask who. Ask God to guide your thinking and talking as a group, and always be aware that you are there to serve people with the gospel, and that the gospel is one of hope and salvation—it really is Good News—and not an opportunity for us to pick holes. Try to see things from their angle too. It could well be that some of the things about the world which make your audience angry, are things which make God angry too. Tell them that, and tell them that God is the only answer. You know that he is the only one powerful enough to defeat the evil in the world because he is the only one powerful enough to defeat the evil in you.

Try wherever possible to sensitively apply Jesus' teaching to people's lives without blunting the message. For example, let's say you decide to retell one of Jesus' stories. For the residents of the old people's home, you might present 'The Story of the Prodigal Grandad' in which Arthur Chambers, O.A.P., F.O.G.E.Y. (and Bar) suddenly realizes that he's let the domino team down by spending all morning at the bookies, so missing the Big Match. Will the team captain, who lent him the money, ever forgive him?

In your school or youth club perhaps football is the thing everyone's into, or breakdancing. Try and use these (wherever physically possible!) as images through which you can deliver your message.

Finally, you can see that we need to use cheek, skill, observation, humour, sympathy and many other abilities which God has given us in order to deliver the message to his chosen audience in a dramatic way. But that will all be useless unless we actually know the person we are talking about, and are constantly allowing him to teach us how to understand the Bible and how to handle it. So make that a priority in your group—to learn, so that you can teach others.

If we've chosen our audience and committed ourselves to being open-hearted in learning how to get to know and communicate with them, then the next thing we need to consider is how we actually go about creating sketches, and what to do with those sketches when we've got them. That's in the next chapter, but before that, I think I need a cup of tea. Excuse me.

Now, suitably refreshed, we move on....

Chapter 4

Gettin' yer act together

Making, Rehearsing and Directing Sketches

In chapter two, we tried to figure out where our starting point for making up sketches should be, and we also went through the points for and against even bothering to produce home-grown scripts. I hope by now you've cottoned on to the fact that we think it's a good idea to try inventing your own sketches. Before our tea break we also looked at the way our choice of audience should affect the style and content of our sketches and the places we can look for inspiration. So much for the brain-work. In this chapter we're actually going to get our hands dirty....

Making sketches

How do you actually make up a sketch?

This is a tricky question because sketches are invented in all sorts of ways. One person, two, three or ten people may be involved in the process. Sometimes the sketch will be written down first and then acted out, but sometimes it will never be written down. In fact, just about anything goes in making sketches, so long as the people involved are happy with the outcome, and the audience enjoys the performance. That's why I've used the words 'making' and 'inventing' to describe the process, rather than 'writing' or some other term. Having said that though, there are two main ways of producing sketches or plays, and a mixture of these two methods is frequently used in creating drama for the television, theatre or for Saturday lunchtime performances outside Woolworths. So, to begin with, it will probably help to describe these two methods as simply as possible.

1. Improvisation

Don't be scared by the word; all it means is 'making it up as you go along'. When this method is used in its purest form, nothing is written down to begin with, and no written script is produced at the end. Somebody just starts acting on an idea for a character or situation with no pre-planned story or conclusion in mind. The others in the company then join in as best they can and begin to introduce ideas of their own. Gradually, characters and relationships between characters begin to emerge, a string of events take place which develop into a bit of story (perhaps through the characters conflicting with each other) and hopefully, after some time the drama reaches some kind of conclusion.

Needless to say, there is no way you can predict what that conclusion will be. Neither can you tell what events will lead up to the conclusion, how long the drama will last, or how good it will be. All these things are left to chance, so an improvised performance can be quite exciting: even the actors don't know what will happen next! However, there are obviously lots of disadvantages with improvisation from a Christian's point of view. After all, the very strengths which some would see in the method—for instance, that anything can happen, that no particular message is conveyed, that it can last for five minutes or five hours—are disadvantages to anyone who wants to use drama to communicate an idea or belief. But that's the extreme version.

Improvisation can be made more practical and constructive for our purposes by setting a few limits on the process. Instead of leaving everything to chance, the company can decide on a theme beforehand and perhaps decide on an 'event' that will start the drama off as well. For instance, the sketch or play could begin with the title 'The Preston Gold-Rush'. All the actors could then imagine how different people would react *the day after* gold nuggets had been discovered in Ribbleton, a few miles outside the city. The group might also decide to limit the action a bit more by declaring that the story will be told from the view point of a newspaper office or a launderette in the city centre, and might even decide what sort of characters are present. For example, a big loud-mouthed editor, a young but enthusiastic tea boy, a glamorous female journalist (who, incidentally, is madly in love with the tea boy) and a police officer who just happened to be passing through in search of his lost sniffer dog. (What they are all doing in a launderette is your problem.) The group might even decide on a conclusion to work towards.

All these 'limits' will help give an improvised drama a bit more sense of direction, while still leaving plenty of room for on-the-spot invention and humour. By repeating the process several times, a basic story can be developed into a definite sketch which can then be rehearsed. In this way some really good drama can be produced.

Nevertheless, it's true that some of the problems mentioned above are likely to remain: a lack of well thought out structure (and with it a tendency to ramble), a 'looseness' of meaning, and the simple fact that many people find it impossible to think on their feet, will prove to be difficult obstacles to avoid without resorting to the second method at some point.

2. Writing

At the other extreme to pure improvisation, is a figure with a very gaunt-looking face and waxy complexion. Onto this face is fixed a sniffling nose which in turn supports a pair of battered specs. The mind behind the specs operates in a body which sits alone, hunched over a pile of paper in a bedroom—or preferably an attic, broom cupboard or similar. Cobwebs stretch from the body's knees up to the desk in front and across to the door frame. Time passes. There is still no movement. It's getting hard to tell whether this is a snapshot or a trendy film. Around the feet of the chair, like a thousand moons surrounding a single star, lies ball upon crumpled ball of discarded paper.

Suddenly—a stirring in the air. Steam pours from

the figure's nostrils—or was it the ears?—as both wrist, and pen-gripping fingers burst into action. It is... *The Writer* at work. Although given to bouts of anxiety and self-doubt, there lurks behind those obsessive eyes the deep-rooted conviction that he or she is an undiscovered genius. All that is produced is perfect. Nothing can be changed without a great deal of heartache and, anyway, actors should stick to acting and not meddle with things they don't understand....

Now, if *The Writer* is a good writer, then he has certain advantages. The scripts produced by a good writer will have precisely what improvised sketches tend to lack: a tight structure which helps the audience to feel that the sketch is actually going somewhere; good, consistent characters who say lines that seem natural enough for those sort of characters; and a good beginning and ending. The message, if the writer has one to deliver, will come out loud and clear but will be 'written in' in such a way that the sketch remains a sketch and doesn't become an illustrated sermon or lecture. So there are some advantages, even if it is difficult to tell whether the writer is dead or alive when you take him his eighth cup of tea! There are more practical problems, too, though.

One is that *Writers* (as opposed to writers) tend to write in a vacuum—only their ideas are considered and used, and they don't feel the need to bother about the practicalities of performing the masterpiece in question. Tender love scenes are OK, but if there aren't any girls in the group, it could be a bit awkward. And stage directions like: 'Space ship emerges through floor (centre stage) and opens to reveal two dozen, three-legged martian warriors,' might prove a bit too testing for the two actors in the group.

The Writer who throws up his hands at any protest and simply replies, 'That's your problem—I am a *Writer*,' is likely to find himself writing from a hospital bed before too long.

There is also the problem that the sketches produced can rely very heavily on words, with very little action, when action is supposed to be what drama is chiefly about. Finally, the other members of the group may find it a bit frustrating if they never get a say in the drama they perform. After all, they've got ideas too, even if they aren't very good at writing them down. But again, *The Writer* is an extreme.

Eye of newt and toe of frog

As suggested before, most companies find a solution to these problems by using a mixture of improvisation and writing—a mixture which will differ from group to group and from time to time. For instance, let's say a professional theatre company have been invited to produce a play on a particular theme, and let's suppose they like using improvisation. In order to improve the final product, they might invite a trusted writer to sit in on their initial discussions and improvisations. After a while, the company would ask the writer to go away and begin writing a script, bearing in mind the facts, ideas and characters that were used, or which emerged, in the group improvisations. The writer would return now and then to consult the group about any difficulties which cropped up, but would eventually produce a provisional script. Providing the script was up to scratch, the company would then begin rehearsals in earnest, recalling the writer if they came to any bits of the script which were hard to understand or difficult to dramatize, or if the company wanted to make any changes to the lines.

Alternatively, a writer might write a script on a theme of his or her own choice with a particular actor or group of actors in mind. They might do this with every intention of allowing the company to add any discoveries made in rehearsal or any ideas of their own to the script although, again, the writer would probably want to be consulted on any changes to the text.

Whether the idea for the play begins with a group's improvisations or in a writer's head, this practice of combining writing and improvisation obviously requires a lot of understanding and tact on both sides. It also has problems of its own, as there is no guarantee, for instance, that the writer and the company will be able to reach any agreement. Despite these difficulties, though, the strength of combining the two methods are enough to make the effort worth while.

Fortunately, in our situation there is every likelihood that agreement will be reached because our primary aim—whether we are writing, acting or both—is to communicate God's truth, and also because as Christians we are committed to being submitted to one another—as we've already seen.

These things should make us doubly intent on reaching agreement, and doubly able to reach it, too.

Back to Back's 100% foolproof blueprint for
producing brilliant sketches every time*

In Back to Back street, I do most of the actual script writing, but everyone else has plenty of room to suggest ideas, characters and so on. And I am involved in the acting, too, which makes me a bit more practical

*Actually, that's not true—Ed.
**But we thought you wanted to sell this book—B to B.

when trying to write a sketch: I tend not to write in too many conversations in Swahili in case I have to do it.

Our sketch-making process usually goes something like this:

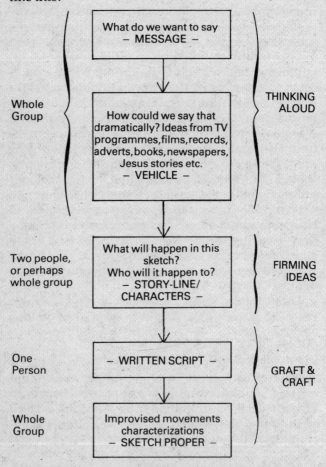

Whole Group — THINKING ALOUD

What do we want to say
– MESSAGE –

How could we say that dramatically? Ideas from TV programmes, films, records, adverts, books, newspapers, Jesus stories etc.
– VEHICLE –

Two people, or perhaps whole group — FIRMING IDEAS

What will happen in this sketch?
Who will it happen to?
– STORY-LINE/ CHARACTERS –

One Person — GRAFT & CRAFT

– WRITTEN SCRIPT –

Whole Group

Improvised movements characterizations
– SKETCH PROPER –

If the diagram doesn't immediately make you think, 'Ugh—Maths, Physics and Biology,' and send you running from the room clutching your head, and/or stomach, you'll notice that in our case 'thinking aloud' in the group and bouncing ideas around is normally the starting point. Perhaps one of us has noticed something fresh in the Bible that is really important, or it could be that we've been asked a question in school which could be answered in a sketch. This could form our 'message'—or part of it. As we saw in the last chapter, the style of the sketch is also part of the message.

On another occasion, though, we might all have been watching telly and seen a programme which had a really strong catch-phrase. Everyone in school or around the youth clubs knows the programme, and the catch-phrase has really caught on. Why not use the catch-phrase for the punch-line or theme of a sketch? In that case, the process would be a bit different, with the 'vehicle' coming first, and then we'd have to try and think what we could say through it.

Everyone who has managed to withstand the shock of the diagram will also notice that with Back to Back the improvisation part, such as it is, tends to come fairly late in the sketch making. That's because we always feel better working from a script, even though the scripts we use look like song lyrics to start with: just the words with ideas for scenes and characters but very few stage directions. I always try to imagine the scenes and characters as I am writing, so at the end of one scene I might write:

(cut to supermarket ⟶)

and then I'd write the next lines with that new scene in mind. When the lines are written, we read the script through together a few times and then, if everyone's happy with it so far, begin to improvise the moves, making any necessary changes in the lines as we go along.

It's a good idea to stick as closely as possible to the script you've agreed on as this will force you to be more inventive as you try to create the scenes it contains, but the key here is to *use* the script. Try doing it several different ways and you'll soon discover that a sketch can often work quite well with different characters and at a different pace, with pauses in different places. While sticking to the script as regards its scenes and most of its lines, don't be afraid to add bits that you think of on the spot—if they make the sketch sharper or funnier without distracting from the point too much—or to cut bits out of a speech which is too long-winded or complicated.

I suppose really this way of creating movements and scenes around a script is a bit like putting a song to music: the movements are orchestrated, the lines bent about and spaced out in order to bring out the message behind the words in the most imaginitive and interesting way possible. The characters, too, must 'come alive' and often be larger than life to have real impact on the audience. But beware of having too much impact on each other....

Support begins at home

As I've said before, if you're going to use this kind of method to invent sketches, you need to be understanding. *Beware of steam-rolling.* Your idea may prove to be better than someone else's, but it will never be so good that it's not worth listening to another person's idea at all. And it's possible to be very destructive even with good ideas. As chief pen-pusher, I like nothing more than getting on my own with an idea for a sketch which everyone has been in on, and then coming back a few hours/days/weeks later with a script which everyone thinks is great. On the other hand, there isn't a worse feeling this side of physical pain than having the fruits of your labours shredded before your eyes. Even an unenthusiastic silence can make me curl up inside. After all, the chances are that the same amount of sweat has gone into making a bad script as a good one—often more. Encouragement is what this is all about—emphasize the good things about each other's attempts, while not ignoring the bad things. Make constructive suggestions for improvements and be willing to try things out—if time can be spared—before making cast-iron judgements one way or the other.

Don't leave all the responsibility for producing scripts on the shoulders of one person all the time. Just because he or she can write, it doesn't mean that they are the source of all knowledge, ideas and inspiration, or that they will have all the skills to produce the finished article. Make sketch-making a team effort wherever possible, so that everyone is involved somehow. Maybe you wouldn't call yourself a writer, but can invent a good story-line. In our group that's Ray's forte. He just seems to be able to think up good angles on things. Even if your contribution, apart from a few suggestions about improvements, is to type up the script once written, you will have had a hand in it and added your support in a practical way. Everyone who writes a script likes it better when it's typed up, so make the effort and it will encourage whoever wrote it as well as make it readable for the rest of you.

Apart from being a '100% foolproof blueprint for producing brilliant sketches every time', these are practical ways of going about creating a script, and if prayerfully undertaken will be fruitful. The truth of that is borne out by some of the scripts in this book. I really wish I'd written 'Space Oddity', but in fact it was written by Sue and Ray in the very early days of Back to Back. Neither would say they find writing sketches easy or even enjoyable—to them it's a real struggle. But out of that prayerful struggle they managed to produce 'Space Oddity' and other sketches which God has spoken through with great effect. So decide how you are going to start, and have a go.

Ideas for improvisation

If you have tried improvising before and enjoyed it, or if you feel that improvisation would be the best way for you to work, pick something from Jesus' teaching or St Paul's letters or a particular 'truth' around which to improvise. Having warmed up, set yourself a period of time—say three minutes—in which you will attempt to interpret the theme you've chosen. For instance, it could be Jesus' words about your neighbour. After discussing the meaning of the teaching and the particular points you think should be emphasized, you can begin. You can of course set yourself some more 'limits' by deciding on a brief story line and/or characters, if you like, but keep going for the full three minutes. Then, do the same thing again, using the same passage and the same ideas, without discussing the first attempt in between. Having completed the second three minutes, talk about the things that did and didn't work, the ideas and characters that developed, and why one version worked better than another. You can then use your findings as the basis for more improvisation or a written script.

A book you may find particularly helpful in improvising is one by John Hodgson and Ernest Richards called *Improvisation*. This covers many kinds of improvisation, both as a way of rehearsing and also for use in making dramas. Again Footprints' book is helpful too, especially as their own performances are good examples of the energy and imagination which improvisation can bring to a sketch.

Ideas for writing

If you fancy a stab at writing a script, or find that improvisation by itself isn't producing the results you want, decide on your theme or message as before and then divide into pairs. Each pair will now try to think of a 'vehicle' for the message—that is a way of putting it over in a sketch. They can then either carry on in pairs to write a story-line/script plan, and even the full script if they want to, or alternatively, each pair can return to the group and share their ideas. Then the group can choose one idea to work into a story-line together, later sending one person off to work on the script. Another way is for each pair to swap their idea for someone else's and try to write that idea into a script (the advantage here is that you can mix ideas while still having several sketches on the go at the same time). You will probably find that some people just seem to spark each other off, so make sure you try different pairings and don't just put best friends together.

Finally, there may be some in the group who fancy trying to write the sketch plan and script on their own. That's OK providing they don't mind everyone having their say about the results.

At the end, compare these ideas and scripts by reading them out, and decide how each might be improved. Then if your group is big enough choose a couple of scripts and split the group in two. Each mini-group can after, say, half an hour's work show the others what they've managed to do with the script. Who knows, with a bit of rehearsal, it could be just the sketch you're looking for. If your group is quite small, spend fifteen minutes on each script and then decide which you want to concentrate on.

Brain food

Unfortunately, there aren't really any books I can recommend that tell you how to write scripts, although you may find the section on writing in Riding Lights' *Lightning Sketches* useful. To me, writing is something to do with trying to imagine how two people might think and respond to each other in a particular situation. Sometimes it helps to think of the times you've been in situations similar to the one you are writing about, for instance, on a bus. Do people have to speak loudly or quietly on a bus? What things get in the way or interrupt a conversation on a bus? Think of the sort of conversations you've overheard on the No. 8 on the way to work or school and see how people really talk to each other, and what they talk about. Another trick is to think of films you've seen where the coversations are really corny and make you think, 'Oh come off it, no one talks like that!' If you want the speech in your sketch to be corny, do likewise, if not then ask yourself what the characters *would* say.

More often, where you are dealing with a certain type of character, like a policeman, or as in the 'Right with God' sketch a quizmaster, it's about picking out the sort of words and mannerisms which are typical of that sort of character. In other words, what do all quiz show hosts apart from Les Dawson have in common? Answer: they are very smooth, seem very insincere, make terrible jokes, wear loud ties and foul jackets and earn a great deal of money.

This matter of thinking what is typical of a situation or character is also involved in the second subject of this chapter: directing.

Directing sketches

The director's job is to sit outside the scene or action in order to watch and listen. He will try on the one hand to think of interesting ways of creating a scene, while at the same time, trying to imagine what the audience would understand from what's happening on stage. Would they be confused at this point, because they can't see the person who's speaking, or can't hear what they are talking about? It may be obvious from the way the actors are standing that we are in a petrol station; obvious, that is, as long as you are sitting in the front three rows, but what about the people at the side, or the back of the hall? Would the audience be bored now, because there hasn't been any visual action for the past few minutes? Or would they be embarrassed because that character, who in this sketch is supposed to be as real as the person sitting opposite, is in fact totally unbelievable?

Because we in Back to Back have no one who is not

involved in acting to fill the role of director, we all have to lend a hand, or rather eyes and ears. We do this by making suggestions (not too loudly or rudely) about the bits we are not involved in, or sitting out of parts of a sketch, while still saying our lines. That way we can comment on what the action looks and sounds like. Often we disagree about how a scene should be done. For instance, if the scene was in a shop, with someone at the counter, I might think it would be best to have the counter side-on to the audience so that they can see the customer hand over the cash to the shopkeeper. Someone else might think that's not so important and that we should see the counter from the front, so that we can also see the shopkeeper's face over the shoulder of the customer. Yet another person might think that the counter should be side-on, but that the shopkeeper should say some of his lines to the audience so that they can see his expression change as he pulls out the shotgun and robs the customer, as well as seeing the customer handing over the money.

In this case, we usually end up doing everything four different ways, arguing, and then eventually plumping for one particular way, or compromising and doing it a fifth way. I suppose 'directing by nego-tiation' would be one way of describing it. Needless to say, this is a very time-consuming practice (I wouldn't really call it a method!), but it does at least produce a result we are all fairly happy with, as most of the alternatives have at least been discussed and usually tried as well.

However, although we all chip in during directing, at the same time we recognize that some people are better than others at spotting what things work and what things will cause problems. Sue is particularly good at this, so where possible we will tend to trust her judgement rather than ours.

In groups where there is no one with any more experience than anyone else, or conversely, where there is someone who is a brilliant director, but can't act to save their drama group, it's probably best to give the job of directing a sketch to one individual.

If you've got the job for the moment, then you'll need to spend a bit of time thinking about the sketch and how you can bring the best out of it. If you're not very good at thinking on the spot, then half an hour spent in this way before the rehearsal will be really useful, and it will keep you one step ahead of the rest of the group. It's much easier to make changes to ideas you've already got than to try weighing up all the alternatives when you've no clear idea of what you're trying to do. However, the need to allow room for discussion remains—the director is simply allowed by the rest of the group to have the last word.

Here are some of the things you will need to have the last word on:

Shape

Words alone are unlikely to hold an audience's attention for ever. That's why preachers rarely read sermons, and one of the reasons why we use drama. The overall visual effect of a sketch is therefore very important. Get the group to run through the sketch or scene again, and this time forget what they are saying. Try instead to look at the shape(s) they are making on stage. Does the stage look cluttered? Are some characters hidden behind others when they need to be seen? Are you using all the space you've got, or is nearly all the action concentrated in an area the size of a drain cover? Would it make the scene more interesting (providing there was a reasonable dramatic excuse) if one character was sitting down and another standing on a chair?

This brings us neatly to something which has become known to us as 'the levels'. Do the characters in your entire twenty-minute sketch spend their time standing up, talking eyeball to eyeball? If so, then your sketch has not got 'the levels'. Varying the shape of the sketch vertically—as well as thinking of moves in terms of walking left, right, forwards and backwards—can make a big difference to the visual appeal of a sketch. So if the scene is about groundsmen at a football pitch, instead of having one groundsman cutting the grass and another marking the pitch, why not have one up a ladder fixing the nets?

Economy of movement

One thing which makes a sketch look poorly rehearsed or sloppy is too much unnecessary (and often unintended) movement. This can be very distracting, as you'll see if you watch TV interviews carefully. When the people being interviewed are nervous, or are just not used to being on telly, they often do the weirdest things like: digging their ears out, picking their fingernails, looking away from the camera, or down at their feet when someone else is speaking, and so on. Despite being watched by millions of people, and perhaps saying some very important things, they will now only be remembered in thousands of homes as 'the man who picked his nose on telly', or 'the woman who sucked her teeth'. So make sure your actors become aware of their nervous habits and try to control them. In addition to this, try to allow only movement which is necessary and which both you and the actors involved know is there. Why are they moving in a certain way? If neither they nor you can think of a decent reason why they should move, let them be still. This will have the effect of isolating movement which *is* necessary and will make it that much more powerful. All movement should be deliberate, sharp, rehearsed and usually 'big', that is, a bit more definite and more exaggerated than is 'natural'.

Stillness

As well as isolating other movement, stillness can also be used to emphasize points or, when combined with silence, to signal the end of a scene. When the stillness ends, a new scene has begun. This is particularly useful in a longer piece, such as 'The Ballad of Georgie Tuck', where an abundance of movement and speech suddenly ceases—on several occasions without prior warning. Through this device, the rhythm of a sketch can be emphasized and the attention of the audience maintained. For some useful exercises in stillness, see Geoffrey Stevenson's section of the book *Steps of Faith*, co-written with his wife Judith. Notice how silence and stillness can be used both to draw attention to itself, and also to highlight other movement.

Imaginitive use of people

There is no law in drama which says that all actors must play people. Use actors to create scenes by playing objects such as: doors, chairs, tables, hospital beds, alarm clocks, telephones etc. You can make your drama quicker like this, because there are no props to shift around, and more imaginitive too. Scenes can flow more easily into one another, the element of surprise is always at hand, foot and elbow. Simple mime like turning a door handle, will have to be well rehearsed though in order to be effective.

Imaginitive use of props

Years of having to cart stuff around from classroom to classroom and from van to church hall and back again, have taught us the wisdom of: 'Propless is Good for You!' Wherever possible, we keep props to a minimum. When we do use them, we try to use them in imaginitive ways. Just as people don't have to be used as actors, chairs don't have to be used only as chairs. So in 'Georgie' (again) the only props we use are three chairs, a shopping bag and some ribbons (plus the canvas screen we always use as a background). Of these the chairs are used as chairs, swing doors, a fast-food counter, a park bench and a staircase. One chair is even used as a euphonium for the Salvation Army towards the end. This, like a minimal use of costume, highlights the bits you do use, and forces you to be inventive.

Sounds

Again, there is no reason why the human voice can only be used for speaking. Sound, whether it's in the form of odd words, noises or music can do a lot to build up an atmosphere. For instance, shut your eyes for a moment. Dark innit?

Now in a minute I want you to do that again, but this time imagine that you are in a railway station and I bet one of the first things you'll think of is the noise of the public address system: Bing Bong, followed by something unintelligible.

Noise is an everyday part of our lives and we can

inventively use our voices to create some great sound effects. Music too. You don't need a brilliant singing voice to imitate the music which will help tell the audience that the action has now shifted from British Rail to British Homestores.

We were reminded of the usefulness of sound when we were performing to a group of partially-sighted teenagers a couple of years ago. It wasn't until we started performing that we realized how much our sketches relied on visual jokes and also visual clues to the story—all things which were being missed by our audience. In order to save the day, we instantly began inventing sound effects for everything: doors creaked, smiles turned to laughs, grimaces became sighs, imagined clocks suddenly became alarm clocks. The whole feel of the sketch began to change. You could even try that as an exercise. Invite someone in to watch your sketch, and don't say anything. Just go through mouthing the words if you like, but telling the story with noises. Then see if your 'guinea pig' has understood it. Some of the sounds you discover you may decide to keep because they really add something to the atmosphere you are trying to create.

Character development

This is one of the most difficult things to tackle. As a director it is your job to coax the rest of the group into 'discovering' their character and then to reproduce the character, not only in their voice, but in the way they pause between words, the way they move, and so on. In order to do this you may have to create conditions which make it easier for your actors to get hold of their characters.

You can start by looking at the basic facts about the

character that you know from the script, or which you have decided on. These will include things like, age, nationality, sex, job (or lack of one), wealth or poverty, intelligence etc. Try to get the actor to think how all these things would affect the character's feelings and attitudes, say towards a teacher, policeman, vicar, or towards the subject of growing geraniums. Also, how would they move, how would they talk? In other words, what sort of character are they? Then if that doesn't seem enough, a simple improvisation or game can be used to help the actor 'find' or invent the individual character or personality that will enable them to make this figure appear believable.

If someone has to portray an old man, for instance, and they can't get the hang of it, ten minutes of rehearsal time could be used to get everyone imagining that they are in an old people's home. In particular, get them to practice how to walk in a way that tells you straight away that they are very old. This will probably lead much more quickly to a convincing portrayal, voice and all, than an hour spent trying to persuade the actor to talk differently. It also helps take the pressure off them a bit. It's very easy to get frustrated when a character doesn't immediately come good and to end up saying, 'I can't do it.' Finding an alternative route to the character which everyone can join in on will prevent them thinking that everyone is watching them and that they are holding everyone else up. Also seeing others who are more able actors or, on the other hand, seeing people make a bigger mess of it than they have, might give them a few more ideas of how and how not to go about it. It will also help the others not to get impatient, and to sympathize, as they've had to struggle with the same problems. Frustrated actors often end up yelling, 'I'd like to see you try!', so it's a good idea to give them the chance of seeing everyone try, before they reach explosion point.

Again, Hodgson and Richards' book *Improvisation*, and also Clive Barker's *Theatre Games* mentioned in an earlier chapter will prove useful here. If you're really into it, Stanislavski's book *An Actor Prepares* and others in the same series will prove stimulating reading, but is probably much more advanced than necessary. Likewise, Cicely Berry's book *The Voice and the Actor* is a bit technical, but if voice projection is something you struggle with, this is *the* book on the subject and you could easily incorporate some of the exercises into your rehearsals. Providing you do them consistently they will pay dividends when you hit either the West End or the open streets.

Rehearsing

It's obviously hard to separate rehearsal from making sketches, and even harder to separate rehearsing from directing, since directing is obviously part of rehearsing. However, there are two things that haven't been covered in this chapter so far that concern rehearsal and which are important.

Firstly, rehearsal time always seems tight, so it's important to organize it well. A bit of time spent organizing a rehearsal schedule for your group will make sure that you use your time to the best advantage. So, decide that you will spend this week's rehearsal time on Sketch B, and next week's finishing it off and also brushing up on Sketch A which you all know already. Then write out a time sheet for this week in some detail. It might go something like this:

Tuesday night rehearsal

7.30   Start.
7.40   Everyone arrives—pray for 20 mins.
8.00   Warm up (15 mins).
8.15   Read through script again (10 mins).
8.25   Rehearse Roger and Steve's parts, while others make props/brush up lines (20 mins).
8.45   Coffee.
9.00   All in on sketch (has Karen organized music?)—ordinary pace/speed run if time (20 mins).
9.20   Final run through for the night (5 mins).
9.25   Fix extra rehearsal if necessary (Saturday morning). Pray.
9.30   All out! (Key back to John's dad.)

Obviously, this is just a guide, and you will doubtless need to spend longer on some things than expected. Equally obvious, is that prompt starts and hard work are the things which stretch your time the most, so make sure everyone knows what time they should be arriving at the next rehearsal. Be there—or be unprepared!

Keeping the pot boiling

The second point to mention is that although all the things included under making sketches and directing are important for rehearsing, there will probably come a point in your rehearsal of a piece where everyone knows what they *should* be doing—they just need to remember lines and moves, and get more practice at playing their character(s) alongside the others. It's at this stage that rehearsal can get really boring—simply going over and over the same bits, trying to remember lines and getting it all to flow smoothly.

The challenge here is to try and make rehearsal interesting. There is obviously a place for really grafting until it's right, but often people get so worked up and frustrated that they actually get worse. At this point either take a tea break or, more productively, promise yourselves one in ten minutes time. Then run through the sketch three more times.

For the first time, see if you can whisper your way through the sketch, or do it in slow motion, but speak fairly clearly.

For the second time, do it like an opera. Really belt it out in song (mind your throats) with grand gestures and lots of melodrama. This will probably have the effect of reducing you all to fits of laughter, but all the time you will be learning your lines and getting rid of some of your frustrations.

Then, thirdly, have another straight run through and have your tea break. Word-bashes, speed-runs, and also mood-runs (where everyone does their parts sadly, or revoltingly cheery, or very...thoughtfully...) can also be valuable and fun ways of learning parts and relaxing yourselves.

Finally, thank God again for all that you've achieved, and get some sleep. You'll need it—your first performance is on the next page.

Chapter 5

Stroll on!

Performing

CREEAK

I have to admit at the outset of this chapter that none of us in Back to Back are too keen on first performances of new material. No matter how hard we have rehearsed, we always arrive at the performance thinking that if we'd had just one more rehearsal session we would have had it all wrapped up. As it is, the time is about 6.30 p.m. on Friday, with the performance due to start at 7.30. We have arrived at the hall to find that the stage is not twelve feet-by-fifteen feet as requested, but is in fact only eight feet deep, and our stomachs have been churning since 4.30. There is no possibility of more staging and if we perform on the floor in front of the stage no one will see us.

Everyone involved in the organization is very excited about the possibilities the evening holds so, having checked that there is no more staging lying around on the premises, we decide to swallow our pride, set up and make the best of it. This means that one or two sketches have to be 'walked through' on the stage, during which we discover that there isn't room to use the step ladder as we normally do for one of the sketches, so we'll have to make do with a chair instead.

By 7 p.m. Fraser is getting a bit rattled because as well as the problems with the stage, 'the man who does the lights' has only just arrived and has only got two lights anyway. One of these has no bracket. The man is presently trying to fix it to the wall with string. Sue tells Fraser to go and get changed so that he'll stop wandering around scowling and getting in everyone's way. In the changing room, Ray is busy fixing cardboard up at the window because, as Hazel has just discovered, all the helpers are having to use the back door of the hall which means they walk right past the window. Fortunately, the cardboard is soon in place and virtue maintained.

Meanwhile, the pastor of the church whose hall is being used for the evening, wants to be introduced to the group and the man on the door wants to know when he should open up—before or after the local kids have kicked the door down.

'At least the publicity's worked,' says Hazel, who is warming up by trying to touch her toes.

'Yeah, I thought it was pretty good,' says Ray who is succeeding.

'Huh,' says Fraser, who is not chuffed, especially as

mid-way through trying to touch *his* toes he has discovered a hole in his trousers.

'Nobody'll notice that,' says Ray.

'Hmmm...' says Fraser.

'Oh cheer up Fraser for goodness sake,' says Sue, who's been setting up the badge board. 'They'll love it, it'll be brilliant.'

Fraser manages a smile. This is what nervous depressive writers like to hear. 'You think so?'

'Oh no,' says Ray. 'That's why we've just spent two weeks rehearsing it!'

'All right, I'm sorry,' concedes our hero. 'Hey—where's Hazel?'

'Silly question,' says Ray.

'Yeah. I think I'd better go again, too,' says Sue and shuts the door behind her.

7.15 arrives. We pray together with some of the helpers, asking God to speak through what we're doing—and to help us get it right.

At 7.35 p.m. the organizer steps on stage to tell a joke. No one laughs. Then he introduces us, casts an anxious glance at the lighting man who is still struggling with the string, and leaves the stage. Overloud cheering from the audience erupts as we take his place. The kids in the audience are obviously intent on enjoying themselves whatever happens. It sounds more like a football match than a concert. We go straight into a sketch designed to catch them by surprise and shut them up a bit. It works. At the end of the sketch, more overloud applause and cheering which eventually subsides and Sue welcomes them all, tells them about the badges we have for sale at the end and introduces the next sketch which is the new, longer one. And amazingly they listen—apart from a crowd of kids on the right hand side who are cat-calling at Ray, and adding their own lines to the sketch. The performance itself is a bit shaky—there are one or two hesitations which only we would know about, and Fraser trips over a few words near the beginning, but apart from that it's OK and the kids' applause seems a bit more from the heart than from sheer excitement, as was the case before.

The rest of the evening goes pretty well too. A row of about seven kids get up and leave about half way through (to go to the disco, we later discover), but the rest clearly enjoy it and are even quite quiet when Hazel stands up and underlines the fact that, although the characters in the sketches are made up, all of us in Back to Back really do have God actively involved in our lives, and so can they if they repent of the way they've left God out of things up till now—and of the things they've done which have really hurt God—and accept the forgiveness which Jesus died to give them. She goes on to say that God will put his Holy Spirit into their lives to give them the bottle to admit they've joined Jesus' followers, and also explains how the Holy Spirit changes us from the inside to be more like Jesus. She emphasizes that life as a Christian won't be easy by referring to one of the sketches, and then says that anyone who *does* want to give their life to Christ can do it tonight. Suddenly there's a real hush about the place.

'If you want to do that, then I'm going to pray for you and then we'll have a few more minutes of quiet. If you want to give your life to Jesus, then I want you to come down here and stand at the front of the stage. Jesus called most of his followers *publicly* and that's what you'll be doing—showing God and everyone else that you're not just mucking about, but you really do want to be a follower of Jesus.'

There's a lot of shuffling, a few giggles and nudges —but there's a kind of sheepishness about most of the kids that shows they're really wrestling with what Hazel has said—a message which they may have heard several times that past week through sketches and discussion in classes, or at the youth club. On this occasion, though, no one walks forward. Hazel doesn't drag it out too long, but says that if anyone wants to talk afterwards they can do.

The concert is over, the snack bar is open, the badges go like hot cakes and someone nicks a book from the bookstall. Quite a few kids come up to talk to us and five—all made aware of their position by the fact that they couldn't go forward—actually decide they want to give their lives to God and become Christians. Often there have been more than this; whereas sometimes no one has come to God, as far as we know. With these five we talk through what commitment to Jesus means for them individually, and what it may mean for them as a group. Individually they admit their sin, ask God to forgive them, thank Jesus for dying in order to make that forgiveness possible and ask God to fill them with his Holy Spirit. We then pray for them, and God *does*. They go away a bit dazed, clutching books in their hands which will hopefully help them to read the Bible and begin to understand more about what's happened to them. They have begun to get to know Jesus.

We are really encouraged by all this because when asked what made them decide that they wanted to give their lives to God, some of them refer to things we said in the sketches—one even mentions the new sketch and says it was exactly what she didn't want to hear! One of the lads recalls something we'd said in his lesson and says that ever since then it had been stuck in his mind. All these people will ideally be put in a local 'nurture group' where they will be helped as much as possible to grow in their new faith, and encouraged to join the school Christian Union (if there is one).

Apart from these five, several kids ask for booklets telling them more about Jesus. Another couple of people ask us to pray with them: one is a Christian, who, as she puts it, has just been going along with everyone else at school, while living a very different life at church. Some other kids, who we really thought would come forward, for some reason didn't, and left straight afterwards.

As well as being excited by the evening and all that God has done, we are exhausted, and also tinged with sadness about all those who still haven't given God a chance to show them how good his life is. Still, we have only seen the immediate results of God's working through us, and we also know that our sorrow can be nothing to what God feels for everyone who holds out on him.

Fortunately, a couple of helpers are on hand to aid us in our exhaustion, and together we put the screens and the rest of the gear in the van. We say goodbye and drive off in search of a cup of coffee and hopefully something to eat as well. Over a coffee and a bag of chips we talk about the evening, telling each other what happened with the different people we talked to and/or prayed for, and laugh about the revolutionary string-held lights that are sweeping the theatre world.

That is how a typical performance for us might go. On other occasions there might be a much wider age range. We might also be working alongside another evangelist who would preach for about half an hour at the end, and there might be a band or solo artist as well. In that case, we'd do less performing ourselves— and we'd have to negotiate with the band about stage space, arranging to move our gear at certain points in the programme so that both groups will have as much space as possible. There might also be plenty of locals on hand to counsel people at the end, in which case we'd just talk to the kids at the snack bar. In another place, a straight performance might be all that is required and appropriate; the drama can speak for itself, so that's OK. We'll just make sure we are around at the end to talk informally to anyone who wants to, whether it's about the drama, how we operate as a group, or about our faith.

Lessons

Hopefully you'll have noticed from this account that when you're performing as a group, you've got to be willing to change your plans to accommodate others (as far as is practical), be aware of the need to encourage each other, and be sensitive to what is right for the occasion. To help you do this in your performances, and to help you do all you can to make your performances as good as they can be, here are a few things to think about.

Organization

The blow by blow account above, mentioned publicity, lighting, staging, refreshments, props, changing rooms, costume, timings, other people taking part, audience, venue and so on. some of these will be important whatever the occasion e.g. staging (or at least space), props and costume. All of them can be checked beforehand. For instance, the trouble with the lighting would not have occured if:

(a) We had been able to carry our own lighting.
(b) We had been more specific about what lighting was required.
(c) If we had arranged for the lighting man to arrive earlier.
(d) If we had not need to use lighting at all.

Even things which aren't usually your responsibility (e.g. publicity, if you are performing at an event organized by someone else) can do with checking. How much publicity will there be? Where will it be placed? Answers to these questions will give you an idea of how many people you can expect in your audience, and the likely age range. What percentage (very roughly) will be Christians? Ask the organizers who they are expecting to come.

In planning which, and how many, sketches to do you will also need to know who else is involved, how much time you've got, whether there is an overall theme to the evening, if there is going to be an interval part-way through, what the aim of the event is, and so on. Many groups rehearse their sketches hard, but forget about how they're going to hang together. Will some taped music be needed to play between sketches, or will someone link them together? Decide who, and make sure they know about it.

'By the left...'

The second thing you'll need to think about and encourage in your group is getting yourselves sorted out on a spiritual footing.

It is not helpful, I tell myself, to start moaning the moment I arrive at the venue. At the same time, it may be helpful to be tactfully honest if something about the organization is wrong. It is also helpful to encourage one another and to quietly get on with the things that need doing, trying to cope with problems as they arise as best you can. A certain amount of *self-discipline* is needed here. It's all too easy to panic, which puts extra pressure on everyone else. You also need discipline as a team. Make time to pray together properly before a performance. Five minutes of hurried SOS calls to God immediately beforehand is not really adequate, although it may be useful. Jesus did amazing things for God, and was often rushed off his feet by people demanding this that and the other, yet we're told that he often spent time alone talking with his Father. I always thought that was just a matter of Jesus 'refuelling his batteries', but recently I've begun to realize that many of the things which Jesus did were the result of his first having defeated the Enemy in prayer.

Again, you've probably heard the saying: 'Don't run before you can walk.' It has been said that Isaiah turned that saying upside down, in chapter 40 verse 31: 'They that wait upon the Lord shall renew their strength—they shall rise up on wings like eagles.' *Then*, after that, 'they shall run and not grow weary, walk and not grow faint.'

We need to take time to wait upon God, allowing him to lift us, if you like, to a higher place before we move into action. As we praise him, we begin to see things as they really are, see the Enemy for who he is, and become aware of our real authority.

As children of God we are also soldiers of Christ and Christ has already won the victory in the spiritual world. Our fears begin to melt away as we become aware of God's almighty, victorious power. If we've 'flown' in prayer, we can run and walk on stage (or wherever we are called to fight) with full confidence in God's power to achieve whatever he wants to, through us. Even if no one responds visibly to our message, and even if we go away knowing that we need to rethink our material, we will still have our hope and confidence intact because we know that we have done what God asked of us, in his power, and we can't do any more.

Into the fray

Having organized as best you can, and prepared yourself physically and spiritually as a team, then you are ready to perform—so get out there!

Once you're on stage, move unhurriedly to your positions. If there is to be an introduction to the sketch, one person should deliver it clearly, in a way that draws the audience into what you are going to do. Then, check that everyone is set, and go for it! I mean, really let them have it!—especially if you're starting the whole programme off.

This is Crisp! Sharp! Dynamic! Ouch!!—The end.

If you're doing another sketch, move swiftly into it so that the pace is maintained. Even if it's a slower, more thoughtful sketch, you still need to take the audience with you. If you're only doing one sketch, bow simply to the audience and clear the stage quickly and without fuss. Do this while the audience is still clapping (encouragement, encouragement!) so that the person or act which follows can make the most of the attention which is now focused on the stage.

And rest....

On the other hand, if you are to follow a deeply moving, quiet solo, for instance, you may need to try and prepare your audience a bit more carefully for the coming shock of a live, dramatic performance. You can do this just by telling them that what follows will be a bit different from the programme so far, but that you hope they will relax and enjoy it. Always be sensitive to the mood of the occasion. So long as that mood is positive you will need to view your slot as a contribution rather than a chance for glory. If the mood is one of boredom, disinterest, or of some other more negative flavour, then your performance could be a real turning point for the whole event, so be confident in what you do, but also be prepared to be the bearers of a few shock-waves.

Always be ready to help the rest of the group if they get into difficulty. There is no excuse for not rehearsing well. On the other hand, you can easily 'dry up' and forget your words because of a distraction or a sudden bout of nerves. Help them out if you can by whispering the opening words of the line clearly, or slightly altering the next line if that helps get round the problem. I have printed on my brain for all time the occasion when a friend of mine was destroyed by a fellow 'actor' who, on realizing that my mate had suddenly gone quiet, said in a very loud voice: 'Oh— you've gone and forgotten your lines haven't you! Typical!'

Not the kind of behaviour likely to draw a group

together, or for that matter to witness to the love among you. Actors who know that the people around them on stage will stick with them whatever happens, are much less likely to make mistakes than someone who is petrified of the consequences if he does.

Service isn't just for Sundays

It's important, when performing, to bear in mind what your relationship with the audience should be. The most useful way I have heard to sum up the actor's part of this relationship is as a *servant*. Jesus said, ' . . . whenever you did this for one of the least important of these brothers of mine, you did it to me!' So be a servant to your audience. Yes, you want to tell them the Truth as you have found it. Yes, they need God. But they also need to feel love and see humility. If you have allowed God to soften your heart, you will want your audience to understand and enjoy what is being communicated through your drama because you want them to have the joy and fulfilment of knowing Christ themselves. It is not the audience's responsibility to admit you are right, or to bolster your ego, or to make you feel that you're a really good drama group. I know only too well that we artists, like preachers, are often very insecure people, but we all have to learn to find our security, not in what we do, or the response we get, but in our relationship with God and the knowledge that we are being obedient to him. That's where our feelings of worth should come from—God's love for us, shown in Jesus. It's our responsibility to love, and to serve our audience with the gospel.

Bows and blows (or how to accept applause and cope with criticism)

At the other extreme to the performer who constantly seeks approval from his audience purely for reasons of ego (and even gets angry if they don't respond positively) is the artist who can't accept applause and thanks. In my experience these are fairly thin on the ground since these things are at least signs that we are holding attention and being appreciated. Nevertheless, there are people who struggle with applause, usually because they so intensely desire people to 'get the point' of, or 'show respect' for the message that any clapping, cheering or yelping with delight seems a superficial response. In other words, they can't have got the point, otherwise they'd be on their knees.

Actually it doesn't mean anything of the sort. Some people may miss the point, true. Others may clap because they share the sentiments or beliefs you have expressed. But many more clap out of a desire to say how much they appreciate the way you have 'given' yourself to them, and just want to say thank you. So accept applause graciously by bowing and smiling at the end of a performance and listen to their praises if they want to congratulate you personally. Don't keep the glory for yourself, though. Praise God that they enjoyed your work, and thank him for the privilege of being able to give pleasure to people while enjoying it yourself, as well as passing on truth.

Coping with criticism is a much bigger problem for me, especially when it comes straight after a performance. Acting burns up a lot of nervous energy, and you will probably find that you are speechless when faced with criticism just after a concert, and then fly off the handle in the dressing room. The best way to cope with this kind of situation is to listen to as much as you can, as politely as you can, thank the person for telling you and say that you will think about what they have said. If you already know what your response to the criticism is—because it has come up before and you've given it some thought—then briefly outline your point of view. Whatever happens don't get involved in a long debate. Either change the subject or excuse yourself and forget all about it for the time being. If you feel that the person was really trying to be constructive, talk to the others about it at the next rehearsal. You may find that what seemed like criticism when it was delivered was actually just some helpful advice, mistimed. At any rate, pray about it and get back to the person involved if you think it would help. Explain that you've given their comments some thought, tell them your conclusions and the reasoning behind them. Thank them again, but explain gently that directly after a performance is probably not the best time to raise such a matter.

If on the other hand the criticism was destructive, for instance, someone pins you to a wall and won't let you escape until he has given you thirty reasons why drama is 'of the devil' and cannot possibly be used by God, or a hundred and one reasons why your drama group is rubbish, then just give it over to God. Jesus took similar, and far worse abuse than we'll ever face so he knows how it feels. Ask him to help you forgive the person involved, and to heal any hurt that you feel—especially if opposition of a destructive kind has come from someone you know. Ask him to help you forget it, too. Praise God for all the good things that have happened and all the things you've learned, and ask for more opportunities to proclaim his Good News.

Opportunity knocks

Jesus' last words before he ascended into heaven were these: 'I have been given all authority in heaven and on earth. Go, then, to all peoples everywhere and make them my disciples: baptize them in the name of the Father, the Son, and the Holy Spirit, and teach them to obey everything I have commanded you. And I will be with you always, to the end of the age' (Mt 28:18–20).

There are loads of opportunities for us to proclaim the gospel through drama in the 80s. I think that when Jesus said, 'Go, then, to all peoples everywhere,' or, 'Go into all the world,' as the Authorized Version has it—it was like saying 'leave no stone unturned'. There are many parts of the world where the stone is still unturned. Underneath there are people who desperately need God's love, forgiveness, salvation, healing, and everything else that makes our life with him so complete.

Drama can be a way into some of these places where other means of proclaiming the gospel would be unwelcome or difficult. Schools, special schools, homes for children, homes for the blind and deaf, OAP clubs and homes, centres for the physically and mentally handicapped and the mentally ill, open or council-run youth clubs, hospitals (maybe via hospital radio), local radio, streets and market places, shopping centres, borstals, prisons, social clubs, pubs and many other places could be served with the gospel in this way. Many of these are hesitant about accepting any particular Christian contribution. Most of them are unglamorous and, for the professional company, are unlikely to pay well.

We may have to adopt different styles and methods in order to communicate effectively, yet many church or Christian Union based groups are well-placed to develop links with these institutions in the local area. If your group is just starting, there may be no way you could begin to tackle some of these places or even gain access to them straight away. But hopefully the thrust of this book has been that if we are faithful to God where we are we can begin to turn those stones over and let the light stream in. Maybe it will start in the youth club, or, if you're at school, by offering to do an assembly. If you're at college you could start by doing a Christmas production for the day centre down the road. Hopefully, the ideas in this half of the book, and maybe the sketches in the next half will help you. Please look after the sketches—it's hard to part with them and we only do it because we think you're worth it.

And, finally, wherever you go, remember who sent you, and that he will be with you to the end of the age.

PART TWO

of

Back to Back's

Little Black

Paperback

Book

Note: the last two sketches are much longer, and could be called short plays. (See Part One for considerations of length.)

Right with God

Characters:	ANNOUNCER
	NIGEL FORTUNE (Quiz Master)
	THE LOVELY CHERYL (Hostess)
	MS CAROLINE FARRINGTON-JONES
	(Contestant)
	MR FRANKY CUDLIP (Contestant)
Props:	Chair
	Question cards
	Costumes to suit characters

This sketch has been one of the most popular in our repertoire for a long time, partly because the quiz show format is instantly recognizable to a very wide age range, and also because people love Franky. He's a classic fall guy really, but in this case he comes out on top. From our point of view the sketch has also been invaluable because the format allows us to give a very clear and direct presentation of facts i.e. the steps you need to take to get right with God.

ANNOUNCER: And now, ladies and gentlemen, can we have a big hand for your host—Mr Nigel Fortune.

    (Applause hopefully! Enter NIGEL.*)*

NIGEL: Hello and welcome to *Right with God*, coming to you live from St George's School, here in Newtown. *(Substitute with appropriate name of venue.)* Tonight we have with us two contestants: Ms Caroline Farrington-Jones, a horse-breeder from Buckinghamshire, and Mr Franky Cudlip, a banana straightener from Wolverhampton. As usual each contestant will be subject to one round of questions to discover if they can be 'Right with God'. And to bring on our contestants tonight, let's have a big hand for the lovely Cheryl...!

    (Applause. Enter CHERYL.*)*

NIGEL: Hello Cheryl. Would you like to give us a twirl please? *(She does.)* Lovely, would you bring on our first contestant please.

    (Exit CHERYL.*)*

NIGEL: Ladies and gentlemen, would you please put your hands together and give a very warm welcome to Ms Caroline Farrington-Jones.

    (Enter CAROLINE, *accompanied by* CHERYL.*)*

NIGEL: Hello Caroline, if I may call you that, and welcome to *Right with God*. And what do you do for a living Caroline?

CAROLINE: Well, actually Nigel, one breeds horses.

NIGEL: Isn't it great, ladies and gentlemen? She breeds horses! I bet you get a kick out of that, eh Caroline? Well, let's get on with the show shall we; if you'd like to take a seat please Caroline....

CAROLINE: Oh, and where shall I take it Nigel?

    *(*CAROLINE *breaks into peals of very 'horsey' laughter.* NIGEL *and* CHERYL *swop exasperated glances and*

push her down onto the chair. CHERYL *passes* NIGEL
the question cards.)

NIGEL: You have just two minutes to answer the following questions, just two minutes, starting from
...now. I am long, I am high and I have a pointed
roof. What am I?

CAROLINE: A church.

NIGEL: Correct. If you saw a man wearing a white
collar, what would it signify?

CAROLINE: That he was a vicar.

NIGEL: Correct. I dress in red and white and I perform
an important function at least once a week. What do
I do?

CAROLINE: Sing in a church choir.

NIGEL: Correct. Could you give me the times of your
local services please?

CAROLINE: 10.30 a.m. and 6.30 p.m.

NIGEL: Correct. What does kneeling with your hands
together and eyes closed signify?

CAROLINE: An attitude of prayer.

NIGEL: Correct. How many books are there in the
Bible?

CAROLINE: Sixty-six.

NIGEL: Correct. Where was Jesus born?

CAROLINE: In Bethlehem... of Judaea.

NIGEL: That is the correct answer Caroline. Is man
perfect?

CAROLINE: Pass.

NIGEL: Do you accept that you have done wrong, that
Christ died to set you free and that you need to give
your life to Christ? Answer 'yes' or 'no'.

CAROLINE: Pass.

(CHERYL *makes a whooping noise to signal end of
round.)*

NIGEL: Thank you, Caroline, your time is up. You passed on just two questions. Is man perfect? The answer is 'no', 'For all have sinned and fallen short of the glory of God,' and the answer to the last question should have been 'yes'. Thank you, Caroline. If you'd like to step into our magic box please.

(Exit CHERYL and CAROLINE behind screen.)

NIGEL: We can now move into our second and final round. Ladies and gentlemen, would you please give a very warm welcome to Mr Franky Cudlip.

(Enter FRANKY, who is very stupid, accompanied by CHERYL.)

NIGEL: Hello Franky. *(No reply. FRANKY stares at audience and laughs stupidly.)* If you'd like to take a seat please Mr Cudlip.... *(Again he just laughs.)* If you'd like to take a seat please Franky.

(More stupid laughter. NIGEL and CHERYL, again losing patience, push him onto seat.)

NIGEL: You have just two minutes to answer the following questions, starting from...now. I am long, I am high and I have a pointed roof. What am I?

FRANKY: Deformed.

(NIGEL is at first angry, but seeing audience laughing plays the showman and joins in.)

NIGEL: Ha Ha very clever, Mr Cudlip. Second question. If you saw a man wearing a white collar, what would it signify?

FRANKY: A pain in the neck.

NIGEL: *(Embarrassed.)* Well many of them are Franky, so I'll give you that one. I dress in red and white and I perform an important function at least once a week. What do I do?

FRANKY: Play football for Arsenal.

NIGEL: O really! Can you give me the times of your local services please?

FRANKY: Well the No. 23 runs along the end of our road every ten minutes....

(He is deftly hit by NIGEL.)

NIGEL: *(Getting more and more angry/embarrassed.)* What does kneeling with your hands together and eyes closed signify?

FRANKY: Err....

NIGEL: I'll have to hurry you up Mr Cudlip.

FRANKY: Pass.

NIGEL: How many books are there in the Bible?

FRANKY: One.

NIGEL: Oh good grief. Where was Jesus born?

FRANKY: In bed.

NIGEL: Can you be a little more specific please Mr Cudlip?

FRANKY: With his mum?

NIGEL: Is man perfect?

FRANKY: *(Laughing at himself.)* No.

NIGEL: *(Laughs.)* No he certainly isn't, Franky, well done. Do you accept that you have done wrong, that Christ died to set you free and that you need to give your life to Christ? Answer 'yes' or 'no'.

FRANKY: *(Thinking hard.)* ...Yes.

NIGEL: Correct.

*(*CHERYL *signals end of round.)*

NIGEL: Thank you, Mr Cudlip, your time is up. You passed on just one question, kneeling with your hands together and eyes closed is an attitude of prayer.

FRANKY: Oh yeah, I forgot *(giggles).*

NIGEL: Yes I'm sure you did Franky.

(He pushes FRANKY *off stage.* CHERYL *also exits.)*

NIGEL: Well that's all we have time for this week, ladies and gentlemen, remember the winner receives the prize of a lifetime. So let's ask the lovely Cheryl to bring on the final scores.

(CHERYL *enters with envelope, and then passes it to* NIGEL.)

CHERYL: Ms Caroline Farrington-Jones seven points, and Mr Franky Cudlip three points.

NIGEL: So this week's winner is... (*He opens the envelope which* CHERYL *has passed to him and is astonished*) Mr Franky Cudlip....

FRANKY: (*Poking his head round the screen.*) Me?

NIGEL: Yes—according to this, Franky, you win because the questions you got right were the only ones you needed to get 'Right with God'. Well done, Franky.

(NIGEL *puts arm round* FRANKY. *They go to bow.* FRANKY *giggles and is hit on the head by* NIGEL. *They bow.*)

Strictly entre nous

Characters: A & B (The two 'natures' of Alan West)
                    A volunteer from the audience

Despite its arty title, which means 'between ourselves', this sketch is very simple, consisting of two actors portraying either 'side' of Alan West. The actors are joined together with ropes around their ankles and also round their wrists, the general feeling being of a battle. Although the sketch is not rooted in any particular scene or situation, the audience's identification with the struggle and their fascination with the synchronized speaking has proved enough to hold the attention of the most rowdy audiences.

Needless to say, the sketch needs careful rehearsal. The secret is for one actor to cue the other by breathing in sharply at the beginning of each phrase, so that they begin precisely together on all parts marked A & B. With lots of practice this can become so subtle and the timing so 'together' that only a very sharp eye can detect it from the audience. If you want the scriptural 'starting point' for the sketch, read Romans 7 as a group. Then, maybe, by talking about your varying experiences of the struggle, a different sketch idea will emerge.

This script contains the barest minimum in the way of stage directions as it is best to make up your own synchronized movements to suit the dialogue.

(The volunteer is seated on a chair at the front right of the stage or playing area—[there's generally no need to tip them off about what will happen].

A *[wishful thinking]* has B *[human nature]* on his left. They begin to struggle by pulling on the ropes.)*

A & B: Will you stop it! Hello. Look! Hello. I expect you're wondering what's going on. I only wish I knew. I'm Alan West...I'm Alan West. Look, don't listen to him. I'm Alan West and I assure you I've never had this trouble before. I wake up, usual time, ordinary day and I'm stuck with him and he claims he's me. I am! Oh for goodness sake, we can't both be Alan West can we. Can we? Yes. Look—we'd better sort this out or they won't understand what's going on. I'm not sure I do. Let's be civilized. We'll each have to tell them our side of the story, right? Fine. You first. Well it's like...oh, part one first then. OK. Right. I'm Alan West...

A: Part 1.

A & B: And I'm Alan West...

B: Part 2.

A & B: Part 1 is...

A: Wishful thinking—I do what he wants to do.

B: But I don't let him

A & B: Because part 2 is

B: Sinful nature.

A & B: Simple *(to audience).* Simple my foot, not to mention embarrassing. Poor things, they haven't got a clue what's going on. Of course they have. You don't think it's just you do you. It's the same for everyone. Really? Yes, it happens all the time.

B: You want to do what's right...

A: And you won't let me.

(Pause.)

106

A & B: I don't understand it. It never used to be like this. Yes it did. No it didn't. Yes it did. No it didn't. Yes it did. You never noticed that's all.

B: Thanks to me.

A & B: What? Nothing. *(Pause.)* First sign of madness you know. What is? Speaking to yourself. You should know. Huh. Hark who's talking. *(Pause.)* Oh, this is useless. I'm off. You want to go? Yes. Now. Well at least we've agreed on something. Come on then. Let's shake hands with *(name of volunteer)* and go. Shake hands? Why not?

A: Friendly gesture.

A & B: OK. Sorry about all this *(to volunteer)*. *(A shakes hand, B slaps head.)* You idiot what did you do that for? It wasn't me.

B: Oh yes it was.

A & B: I really am very glad I did that. No I'm not. Will you shut up! Not you *(name of volunteer)*. Oh good grief this is getting worse. I wish I could get rid of you! I'm very sorry. I assure you it won't happen again.

B: *I* wouldn't be too sure of that if I were you.

A & B: Oh belt up!

 (They gesture that the volunteer should sit down again.)
(To audience.) It's been like this all day. I've lied to me dad, swore at me mum, split on me best friend and nicked two quid off me brother!

A: I knew it was wrong even when I was doing it.

B: *(With glee.)* But I still did it.

A & B: I know, I wish I could get rid of you.

B: But you can't get rid of me—not by yourself.

A: What was that?

A & B: Nothing.

A: *(Thinking.)* Not while you're on your own.... That's it!

B: What?!

A: Come on!

B: What are you doing?

A: I'm going to get rid of you.

B: Over my dead body!

A & B: Exactly!

 (They freeze, pointing at the audience.)

Transfer

Characters: DOREEN (Northern Mother and trainer)
TOM
DICK
HARRY (or Harriet)

Props: Whistle
Headscarf
Shopping bag
Telephone
Handbook

This is a very simple sketch which works equally well inside or out. It illustrates both our failure to live up to God's perfect standard, and also how Jesus' dying in our place has made it possible for us to receive the Father's forgiveness and be reconciled to him. We are 'transferred' from the hopelessness of life without God to the 'first division' of life with him.

Needless to say, football language is familiar to many people, and Doreen's ability to talk directly to the audience makes the sketch quite engaging. It can also cope with the responses of audiences in the street, who tend to be far less restrained than those sat in a church hall or classroom. In addition to this, the abundance of movement provided by the exercises, and the comedy of seeing the characters (and the actors) trying to do them, keeps the sketch from being too 'heavy'.

It is *vital* to do some warming up before even attempting to rehearse this sketch, and if you're not very fit, allow at least two days after the performance to recover!

(Enter DOREEN, *who takes up position at the front of the playing area or stage. She blows her whistle and is followed by* TOM, DICK *and* HARRY, *running on the spot in a row behind her.)*

DOREEN: C'mon you lot, get them knees up. C'mon, higher! One, two....
*(*TOM, DICK *and* HARRY *do an exercise e.g. arms outstretched to side, and legs together, in time with each other and with Doreen counting.)*
DOREEN: ... Three, four, five. Now—squats. One, two.... *(On the second one they freeze.)*
DOREEN: *(To audience.)* No doubt you're all wonderin' what's goin' on 'ere. Well, this is Tom, Dick and Harry, and me, well I'm Doreen their mother... three, four, five. C'mon.
(They touch toes.)
DOREEN: One, two.... *(They freeze again.)* Y'see Tom, Dick and Harry play football for Burton Under Water Rangers, Northern Premier League, and they're after a transfer to the first division. Me, y'know I reckon they stand as much chance as a frog in a liquidizer. Still, we'll give it a go. I picked up this handbook from your local library—supposed to be the best there is—and that's what we're workin' through at the moment... three, four, five.
One: *(They do side-kicks three times to the right.)* Thou shalt have no other gods before me.
Two: *(Side-kicks to the left.)* Thou shalt not make unto thee any graven images.
Three: *(Three side-stretches to the right.)* Thou shalt not take the name of the Lord thy God in vain.
Four: *(Three side-stretches to the left.)* Remember the Sabbath and keep it holy.

Five: *(Touch left toes with opposite hands twice.)*
Honour thy Father.... *(Proudly.)* And thy Mother.
Six: *(Touch right toes with opposite hand twice.)* Thou shalt not kill.
Seven: *(TOM and HARRY pick up DICK then lift him up and down.)* Thou shalt not commit adultery.
Eight: Thou shalt not steal.
Nine: Thou shalt not bear false witness.
Ten: Thou shalt not covet. Now, the question is, can you manage all that?

> *(They collapse, exhausted, in a heap.)*

Oh, just as I thought. Y'know they're about as much use as a wet lettuce. The only place you lot'll get transferred to is hospital if you carry on like this.

T D & H: *(In unison.)* Oh Mum—give us another chance will yer—I'm sure I can do better next time.

DOREEN: Oh, I'm not sure.

T D & H: Oh, Mum.

DOREEN: Oh all right then, start again.

> *(They begin running on the spot, blowing very hard and loud, preferably in time with each other.)*

DOREEN: Well, as you can see... hang on a minute.

> *(She blows her whistle and they begin to run silently and in slow motion.)*

As you can see, they didn't get much better, in fact they got so 'tatered they were worse than when they started.

> *(They collapse. At this point, whoever is likely to have the most energy left makes the sound of a telephone ringing. DOREEN, surprised, looks around her then traces the sound to her shopping bag. She opens it and warily pulls out a telephone receiver.)*

DOREEN: Hello...speakin', aye...yes, that's right Tom, Dick and Harry. *(Each lifts his head when he hears his name.*) What?! A transfer?

T D & H: (*In unison.*) A transfer?
(They sit up as they speak.)

DOREEN: To the first division?

T D & H: To the first division!
(They kneel.)

DOREEN: But they're useless!

T D & H: (*Sadly deflated as they stand.*) But we're useless.

DOREEN: (*to* T D & H.) It'll be all right, the training's included.

T D & H: But what about the transfer fee?

DOREEN: (*Listening.*) It's been paid? How much? But they're not worth it!

T D & H: (*Sadly.*) We're not worth it.

DOREEN: Who's paid all that? Says in the handbook. Right. Thank you very much, thank you, 'bye. Says in here who's paid it—we'd better have a look.
(She re-reads handbook and they crowd round.)

DOREEN: (*Reading.*) You are not your own, you have been bought with a price.

TOM: (*Taking book.*)...This includes you who were once far away from God. You were his enemies and were sep...sep...separ....

DOREEN: (*Taking it back.*) Separated...from him by your evil thoughts and deeds, yet now he has brought you back as his friends....

DICK: (*Taking book.*) He has done this through the death on the cross of his own human body.

DOREEN: (*Taking back book.*) And now he has brought you lot into the very presence of God....

T D & H: (*Very proud.*) Hey—Champion!
(They run off stage very elated.)

DOREEN: (*Picking up her handbag.*) Well, who'd've thought it. Be seein' yer. (*Exits.*)

Roundabout

Characters: NARRATOR
              GEORGE HENRY ADAMS
              PREACHER
              MUSICIANS

Props: Rope
              Money bags
              Carnation (flower, not tin of)
              Present
              Teddy bear
              Doll

In most of our sketches we've always tried to show not only the predicament that a world without God is in, but also to at least point in the direction of God as being the only possible source of real help. Sometimes, though, it's useful to simply portray the pointlessness of life without God, and the inadequacy of the various comforts which the Western world in particular offers as a replacement. That leaves the way open for the people who watch to conclude for *themselves* that 'there must be something better'. This is particularly true if such a sketch can be used as part of a series of sketches, or if the sketch is to be followed in an evangelistic meeting, for instance, by a preacher.

That's the line this next sketch takes, and because of its form and subject, it is particularly good for adult audiences—perhaps especially non-Christian church goers (although it may also be a good reminder to Christians of the message of the Parable of the Barns [Lk 12: 16–21], for instance.)

The NARRATOR *stands on a chair in the centre with one end of a rope tied to his/her waist. Within the* NARRATOR'S *reach are all the props—best placed on the chair somehow.*

The other end of the rope is made into a hangman's noose, which is placed over GEORGE'S *neck.*

The MUSICIANS *stand at the rear of the playing area, and sing a fairground tune quietly, almost to themselves. You can also have them banging drums/ cymbals, if you like, but they mustn't distract too much from the action.*

As the action progresses, GEORGE *acts out various fairground games while walking around the* NARRATOR *in a circle. The size of the circle will get smaller as the rope, wrapping round the* NARRATOR, *gets shorter.*

NARRATOR: A life in the day of George Henry Adams. (GEORGE *yawns and stretches.*) Born of poor but honest parents on the fifth of October, nineteen hundred and twenty-seven.

PREACHER: *(Speaking very fast in nasal tones—preferably delivering the whole of each speech in one breath.)* George Henry Adams I baptize you in the name of the Father, and the Son and the Holy Ghost. I sign you with the sign of the cross in token that hereafter you must not be ashamed to confess the faith of Christ crucified and manfully to fight under his banner against sin, the world and the devil and to continue Christ's faithful soldier. . . .

NARRATOR: Educated Springfield secondary modern, did rather well at sport—centre forward in the first eleven *(coconut shy)*. . .right back in lessons. Left school 1941, first job machine operator, saved. . . *(test of strength hammer—wins)*. . . and was soon able to buy his first motor bike—a Honda 50. Summer 1947 *(bowls)* bowled over by the beauty of a blue-eyed blonde. The stars were bright, her touch was light, the music was soft, the scent of the flowers did waft across the warm evening air, a nightingale sang—bells rang: ding-dong, ding-dong, ding-dong.

(NARRATOR *throws* GEORGE *a doll, preferably with a miserable face.*)

PREACHER: George Henry Adams, wilt thou have this woman to be thy lawful wedded wife, to live together according to God's law in the holy estate of matrimony? Wilt thou love her, comfort her, honour and keep her, in sickness and in health and forsaking all other, keep thee only unto her, so long as ye both shall live?

NARRATOR: And so they were married—the beginning of domestic bliss: *(rifle range)* mortgage, second-hand car, life insurance, washing machine, three sets of casserole dishes, in-laws *(wins a box—wrapped up).*

Soon comes the patter of tiny feet around the house—so they hired Rentokil and blocked up the holes *(hoopla).*

1952—first child, a bonny, bouncing baby boy *(receives teddy bear, wrapped in blanket)* with a nose just like his father's *(show audience bear's face).*

1954—promotion at work—foreman, new car, new house.

1956—new baby—a girl (aaah). For George Henry Adams things are looking good.

1961—redundant *(empty pockets)*...out of work three months. Re-employed *(finds money in inside pocket)*, shop floor inspection.

1965—time for a change *(starts dice game)*. So our friend decides to sell up and begin again as a self-employed man. His very own business—making wrought-iron gates. At last his own boss: freedom! Real responsibility! Job satisfaction! And complicated tax forms. *(He is given a pile of paperwork from* NARRATOR.*)* George Henry Adams is successful, his business expands, his bank balance swells. *(He receives money bags from* NARRATOR *and he is now getting quite weighed down.)*

1968—first child killed, road accident.

PREACHER: We brought nothing into this world and we carry nothing out, the Lord giveth and the Lord taketh away, blessed be the name of the Lord. Earth to earth, ashes to ashes, dust to dust....

NARRATOR: Second business doing very well thank you. Two cars, three-bedroomed detached house, family.

1973—daughter marries—nice lad, with good prospects—double barrelled too. We are moving up in the world. *(He receives a carnation between his teeth.)* Better think about settling down I suppose. Bungalow perhaps? Chairman of the Rotary Club, reproduction furniture, holidays abroad, first grandchild, tupperware parties, world cruise, index-linked savings....

By this time, rope around his neck is quite short. NARRATOR *jerks it upwards and* GEORGE *is hanged, dropping all that he has accumulated. Music also stops sharply at that point. The tableau is held for a few moments, before bowing.)*

N.B. Please rehearse carefully....

Space Oddity

Characters: CAPTAIN BURKE
LIEUTENANT ATORA
MR SOCK
DUMB BLONDE
The voices of MORAG (the computer) and
INTERNATIONAL RESCUE

Props: Cassette Recorder
Items of space-like costume
Console (either free standing or suppor-
ted by a table—suitably painted and

equipped with toilet roll).

In a larger hall a small p.a. system with a microphone behind the screen will help projection of the 'voices'.

'Space Oddity' is the result of years of addiction to science-fiction programmes like *Star Trek*, *Sting Ray*, *Fireball XL5*, *Dr Who* and, more recently (showing ourselves to be not only old but also durable), *Blakes 7*. All these programmes have a lot in common. Besides dreadful costumes, corny sound effects and scenery made out of *papier mâché* sprayed silver, they all have heroes who speak in short, sharp, urgent tones when facing disasters (usually about a dozen per episode). Each episode is also filled with masses of pseudo-scientific jargon like 'matter-projection', 'astro-magnetic force-retractor beams' and 'transmutational alienoids'. So, present the audience with a 'console' (centre stage) and characters dressed in silver Lurex tabards and they'll immediately know what to expect. The challenge is to surprise the audience by using the standard science-fiction imagery to point them towards God and the need for them to make a decision about him.

When rehearsing use your imagination to develop very sharp, stylized movements e.g. head turns, expressions of horror/excitement/stern control etc. Also make the most of the chance to invent sound effects using your vocal chords rather than tapes. Tapes *are* best, however, for the intro music, for example, the *Thunderbirds* theme. You can usually borrow recordings from a library and, providing 'snatches' of music aren't used for performances where there is an admission fee, copyright is not generally infringed.

Finally, the aim throughout this sketch is to send up the space thing as much as possible, so feel free to add lines and substitute characters in accordance with whatever programmes are current, while being careful, at the same time, to maintain the 'thrust' of the piece.

(Intro music of 'Star Trek' or similar is played during which CAPTAIN BURKE, LIEUTENANT ATORA *and* MR SOCK *enter and take up positions. All working on bridge except* DUMB BLONDE. *Noises—bleeps—whirrs etc.)*

CPT. BURKE: *(Intro intercom.)* This is the voyage of the starship Rentapart. Its lifetime mission to boldly go where no man has gone before...recently. Captain's log stardate 021772 6558. Ship approaching the outer regions of the Galaxian Delta 7. Everything seems OK on the screen, but I've got this feeling that there's something strange out there...something weird...*(turns).* Lieutenant Atora....

LT ATORA: Yes Captain?

CPT. BURKE: Any news?

LT ATORA: Negative Captain.

DUMB BLONDE: *(Rushes in.)* Help, help, Captain...you must come to the engine room.

CPT. BURKE: Why? What is it?

DUMB BLONDE: Well, it's this big room downstairs where the engines are kept.

CPT. BURKE: I know that stupid. What's happening?

DUMB BLONDE: The ship's being invaded by glumphy, bog-eyed, girbled magwiches.

CPT. BURKE: Are you sure?

DUMB BLONDE: Sorry—that's next week's episode. *(She exits).*

MR SOCK: Captain there's something on the screen!

CPT. BURKE: What is it?

MR SOCK: Nothing.

CPT. BURKE: But you said there was something.

MR SOCK: That's just it! There's nothing there!

LT ATORA: Oh no, you know what that means.

MR SOCK: Yes.

LT ATORA: We are being drawn

MR SOCK: Towards

LT ATORA: A black

MR SOCK: Hole.

LT ATORA: The inevitable end of every space ship.

MR SOCK: It had to happen sooner or later.

CPT. BURKE: *(Cool.)* Perhaps not. We may still be able to escape.

MR SOCK: That's impossible.

CPT. BURKE: Switch over to manual.

LT ATORA: Manual.

CPT. BURKE: Warp factor ten.

LT ATORA: Warp factor ten.

CPT. BURKE: Touch of the left hand down a bit.

LT ATORA: Left hand down a bit. *(Crew members tilt to the left.)*

CPT. BURKE: Fire retro-rockets one, two, three and four.

LT ATORA: Retro-rockets fired Captain.

CPT. BURKE: Warp factor eleven and increasing.

LT ATORA: Warp factor eleven and increasing. *(Noises....)*

MR SOCK: It's no good Captain, the dilithium crystals are burning out and we haven't enough power to pull away from the black hole!

LT ATORA: This could be the end of civilization as we know it.

CPT. BURKE: Not quite, Lieutenant. It's a long shot, but it might just work.

LT ATORA: You mean....

CPT. BURKE: We need outside help.

MR SOCK: You mean....

CPT. BURKE: Yes.... Calling International Rescue. *(Music—'Thunderbirds' theme—in the middle of bridge synchronized movement imitating Thunderbird puppets driving space ship.)* Hello, International Rescue, this is the Starship Rentapart.

INT. RESCUE: Go ahead Rentapart.

CPT. BURKE: We need help. We're being sucked into a black hole.

INT. RESCUE: A black hole! I'm sorry, but International Rescue is unable to prevent your destruction.

(Noises by DR SOCK *and* LT ATORA.*)*

CPT. BURKE: Hello, hello....

LT ATORA: Oh no. *(Faints.)*

MORAG: Ouch!

LT ATORA: What?!

MORAG: Do you mind getting off my input valve?

LT ATORA: Whoops, sorry.

CPT. BURKE: Of course! The computer! Morag....

MORAG: Yes, Captain?

CPT. BURKE: Can you save the ship?

MORAG: I'm sorry. My circuits are not sufficiently programmed to save the ship. May I make a suggestion?

CPT. BURKE: Go ahead, Morag.

MORAG: In case of black hole, contact the Creator of the universe, freephone 777.

LT ATORA: 777. *(Unrolling toilet roll as a computer print-out.)*

MR SOCK: What does it say?

CPT. BURKE: It says... 'Now wash your hands please.' No, wait, there's more. 'In order to escape death you must hand over complete control to the Creator of the universe. He is the only one able to save you.'

MORAG: Ten, nine, eight, seven, six....

CPT. BURKE: But it's my ship.

MR SOCK: There must be some other way.

LT ATORA: Captain, it's our only chance. You must hand over!

MORAG: Two, one....
(*Explosion! They freeze in blast position for a few
seconds then face front.*)
ALL: Will Captain Burke and his crew be saved? Will
they hand over control to the Creator of the universe?
Only YOU can decide....

The Ballad of Georgie Tuck (or Wossapoint?)

This is a tightly-written, fast moving sketch which, although containing well over a dozen different characters (most of whom are fairly incidental to the story), was written to be performed by just four people. Many of the aims and assumptions which we talked about in the earlier half of the book were first put into practice in 'Georgie', and many lessons which have since been incorporated into other sketches and plays were originally learned through performing this sketch-cum-play in classrooms, school halls, theatres, bars and many similar situations. In fact, it was originally written to be performed in classrooms and other places where you can get very close to the audience and hold their attention by talking directly to individuals, and maybe making jokes at their expense. It's probably in that sort of setting that it has been most successful in communicating, and most enjoyable to perform, too.

To understand how it was written, and why it was written in the way it was, it's worth recapping the limits we set ourselves. Firstly, it had to be between fifteen and twenty minutes long, to fit comfortably into a thirty-five minute, or hour-long lesson and still leave room for discussion.

Secondly, it had to be versatile. We wanted to perform it in lots of different places, so it couldn't require too much space either for performance or props.

Thirdly (one of our original limits), it would have to be funny, fast-moving and interesting enough to hold the attention of people who weren't really interested, either in drama or what they would call 'religion'.

Fourthly, the subject we had decided on. We thought that the question of 'What's the point of living/ Everything's boring' would be the best subject to tackle, since it came up so often in school.

What came out was 'The Ballad of Georgie Tuck'— just a bare script which after two weeks of hard labour became seventeen minutes' worth of performance. It uses very few props in some quite interesting ways; no costume changes (but lots of character—and scene changes), and a central character who can tell his story from his point of view, both as he saw it then and, also, as he sees it now. This enables the central character to both get 'alongside' a non-Christian audience, because he shares their way of thinking in some ways, but at the same time he can shed a bit of light on things because he now sees things a bit differently.

This method of 'reporting' events through a central character has enabled us in this sketch, and others written since, to talk quite plainly about experiences as difficult to tackle as conversion or recommitment without getting bogged down, either in clichèd church-lingo or in lots of self-examination. The character simply says what happened, and what's happened since. Needless to say, theories are usually developed from discoveries made by accident or through trying to cope with necessities.

That's also probably how you will make 'Georgie' work—through trying it out and overcoming the difficulties that arise. It would be impossible to describe all the moves in any detail—you will have to invent each new scene yourselves, and also work out how to move from one to the other. What I can do, is outline the 'doubling up' combination which we found to work for us in covering all the different characters. Apart from that, allow yourselves plenty of time to rehearse, both helping you to get your movements smooth, and also to help whoever plays Georgie to get a real grip on the character. Georgie, by the way, is a Black Country kid through and through, with an accent to match. That also affects some of the expressions he uses, and his way of thinking. If you can't get the hang of the accent (or if listening to the garage-hands in *Crossroads* proves too painful to use for research) then I suppose you could try an accent more local to your area, although some of the phrases Georgie uses may need adapting.

Anyway—all the best.

Main characters:	GEORGIE
	MUM
	DAD
	SHARON

Incidental characters:	NARRATORS A & B
	TEACHER
	TV
	PEOPLE (on bus)
	GOALKEEPER (Georgie's mate)
	SERVERS A & B (in MacDougals)
	THE HUNK
	MODELS (in shop window)
	PARKY (park keeper)
	SALVATION ARMY (CAPTAIN and MARGARET the songster leader)
	CHERYL

In our production, the characters are divided out like this:

> Fraser—Georgie
> Ray—Dad and all incidental characters marked in the script as 'A'
> Hazel—Mum and all incidental characters marked in the script as 'B'
> Sue—Sharon and all incidental characters marked in the script as 'C'

Props:	Three small chairs (infant Sunday School size)
	Red and white ribbons fastened to a curtain ring (for Salvation Army timbrel)
	A shopping bag
	Screen (painted canvas on wooden frame

for background)

Costume: None, other than basic performing strip.

A classroom.

A: Imagine a city.

B: Imagine a school.

A: Imagine a classroom.

B: Imagine a lesson—we thought it might take your mind off things....

A: Imagine a pupil.

B: Imagine a teacher.

A: A boring one...

B: If you can imagine it.

A: But most of all—

B: Imagine Georgie.

A: Not very bright...

B: Bit of a dreamer—

A: But he's all right, is Georgie.

(A *starts to wind up* TEACHER, *as with a starting handle.*)

TEACHER (C): Good morning class 3D. (*Collapses.* A *winds again.*) Good morning class.... (*Again collapses.* A *winds again, and this time the 'motor' catches.* A & B *take seats.*)

TEACHER (C): Good morning class 3D and welcome to today's history lesson.

B: And off we go.

TEACHER (C): Today we're going to learn all about the Norman Conquest....

(*Fades to barely audible rambling about Norman Conquest which continues till the end of the scene, becoming louder at the intervals marked.*)

GEORGIE: They ought to bring back executions. She'd

be the first. History's so boring—all them dates *(has idea)*. Talking of which....

A: Later, Georgie.

GEORGIE: All right.

TEACHER (C): ...and shot Harold in the eye with an arrow....

GEORGIE: 1066—The Norman Conquest. I mean, what's that got to do with me, eh? Do yer know warr I mean? I mean what's the point of teachers? What's the point of school?

A: Georgie is thinking again...

B: ...rather than just learning.

A: Very dangerous.

B: *Very* dangerous.

TEACHER (C): ...can now be seen in the Bayeaux tapestry....

GEORGIE: 1066 and me—I don't get it! Every day I sit here, and sometimes I learn something, but why? What's the point? *(All are still for a few seconds.)* Then, when I get home, me mum'll say....

(Scene is now changing to living room. MUM picks up two chairs. DAD stands in front of TV.)

MUM (B): Oh, you're home then. Want some tea?

(She places chairs down to form settee, and she and DAD sit down to watch TV.)

GEORGIE: And we'll sit down, watch telly, and not say a word. The news, then *Crossroads*, or the film—depending on what night it is, while me mum falls asleep in the chair. Then Dad goes to the pub, and I go to bed. About 11 o'clock, me dad gets back and the beep comes on the telly. Then the telly gets up and turns them off!

TV (C): Beep! *(Switches MUM and DAD off. They sit frozen bolt upright.)*

131

GEORGIE: They stay like that till breakfast, and then they start eating again. Oh well, no harm in hoping, is there?

(A makes sound of school bell, and scene reverts to the classroom.)

TEACHER (C): Class dismissed!

(Scene changes to bus queue.)

GEORGIE: Ah—music to me ears. I suppose, if you think about it, there's not a lot of point to much, is there? Like the bus.... (GEORGIE, B & A *are now standing on the bus.)* Buses, according to the experts, are for gettin' people from A to B, fairly quickly and in reasonable comfort. *(C, as an old woman, pushes between* GEORGIE *and* A, *to sit down.)* Well, they got that wrong for a start didn't they! But what I reckon is this: if everyone who lived in A swopped houses with everyone who lived in B, they wouldn't have to go on the bus to get there. Then they could get rid of all the buses. Mind you...then you'd have nowhere to stick your chewing gum... *(Sticks chewing gum to 'ceiling' of bus, much to the annoyance of other passengers)...*would ya? *(Laughs.)*

(Scene changes to football match. B & C stand on chairs and are gateposts, at the rear.)

GOALKEEPER (A): *(Concentrating on the game.)* 'Ere Georgie—want a game?

GEORGIE: No thanks—I'm off out.

GOALKEEPER (A): Not that Sharon again, is it?

GEORGIE: Ah shurrup....

Take football for instance: twenty-two men, plus an old man, meet in a park to kick a ball about. The object, according to the rules anyway, is for half of the blokes to get the ball between the posts at one end, while the other half are tryin' to get it in at the other end. This you can do anyway you like, as long as the ref. (that's the old bloke) don't see ya. And the winners get to kiss each other at the end! If it's a big game, they get to swop shirts an' all... (GEORGIE *has been wandering across the goal mouth, cutting out the* GOALKEEPER'S *view. His mate has therefore just let a goal in)*...which is a bit pointless really, 'cos next week they're going to do the same thing all over again which means that everyone has to buy a new shirt before Saturday.

(The scene now changes back to the living room at home, with A *now replacing* B *on the chair, and the 'goal posts' becoming the sides and roof of a house.)*

GEORGIE: Forest Road. Ours is No. 16: exactly the same as everyone else's in our road—which is no bad thing, 'cos it means if you go in the wrong house by mistake, you do at least know where the bathroom is.

*(*A *and* B *now become* MUM *and* DAD, C *becomes* TV *as before.)*

MUM: Oh, yer home then. Want some tea?

GEORGIE: No thanks, I've had it two billion times already.

MUM: Eh?

GEORGIE: Oh never mind. *(Watching telly.)* I'm, er, off out tonight, Mum.

MUM: Are you indeed—done yer homework then?

GEORGIE: *(Thinking quick.)* Oh yeah—I, er, did it on the bus on the way 'ome.

*(*GEORGIE *steps onto chair, stage left, as* MUM *and* DAD *freeze, stage right.)*

GEORGIE: The bathroom, like I said, is in exactly the same place as everyone else's in our street. But *ours* is *pink*! Hey, that's nothing to get excited about, I just thought I'd mention it. I'm...er...going to have a shower now so if you don't mind, ladies, we'll skip ahead a bit. *(He pulls the 'curtain' across and freezes. Complete stillness continues for a few seconds before he opens it again and continues.)* Right *(climbs off chair)* comb me hair...spot of 'Bruno'—for the man who doesn't even bother to try any more—and we're all set for a stroll in the park with the delectable Sharon.

(Walking through living room.) See yer later then, Mum. *(No response from* MUM *who is still frozen.)* Mum?! *(He passes hand in front of* MUM'S *eyes. No reaction. Points to telly.)* Ere, it works!! *(Looks at watch and notices the time.)* Cor, I'd better be off!

(Scene changes to street corner. A & B *with backs to audience are still and have dropped out of the action.* SHARON *is in the background.* GEORGIE *has not noticed her.)*

GEORGIE: I've agreed to meet Sharon at the corner of Princess Street by the cafe. She's not bad, Sharon. Not exactly pretty like, but er...all right in a dim light, like—yer know worr I mean?

(SHARON coughs impatiently.)

GEORGIE: Oh hello, Sharon. Bit early aren't yer?

SHARON: You're late!

GEORGIE: Yeah, well I overslept didn't I. Well, let's go shall we...

SHARON: Where we goin' then?

GEORGIE: Well I thought we'd give the flicks a miss tonight—as we've seen it before, and...

SHARON: *I haven't!*

GEORGIE: All right then—as *I've* seen it before, I thought we'd go for a stroll in the park. It's a nice night—knowworr I mean? *(Nudge, nudge.)*

SHARON: Yeah—you mean yer broke, don't yer.

GEORGIE: *(To audience.)* Yeah, well, as it happens very nearly almost.

I've got a *bit* of money though. I thought we'd go for summat to eat later on.

SHARON: Come on then—let's go to MacDougals!

GEORGIE: Wait—Sharon!

(Scene moves into American-type hamburger place. A & B holding chairs, first become swing doors through which GEORGIE and SHARON enter restaurant. They then become servers, also stage right, holding chairs as counter and calling orders over their shoulders. Their yelling continues throughout the scene. SHARON sits down, stage left.)

GEORGIE: American fast-food joint. Plastic food, plastic people and very expensive. Sharon gets to sit down, while I get cleaned out!

SERVER A: OK. Two big Macs and french fries coming up.

SERVER B: *(To GEORGIE.)* Can I help you, sir? Can I help you?

SERVER A: I hope you enjoy your meal....

GEORGIE: *(To SERVER B.)* Yeah—one cheeseburger and one milkshake please. Oh, and two straws please. *(Winks to audience.)*

SERVER A: Can I help you, sir. Can I help you?

SERVER B: OK. One cheeseburger and one milkshake coming up. That's £3 please.

GEORGIE: *(Digging in his pocket for more money.)* And two straws please.

SERVER A: One big Mac, french fries and a crispy pancake roll—£9.75 please.... *(Etc.)*

GEORGIE: They guarantee—in these places—that yer food is ready by the time you get yer change. The

135

catch is, everything is so expensive, you never get any change! Which gives them plenty of time.

SERVER B: OK. Thank you sir—enjoy your meal. Can I help you, sir. Can I help you?

GEORGIE: Excuse me! Excuse me!!

SERVER A: Can I help you, sir?

GEORGIE: Er, no thanks, I'm being served.

SERVER A: OK. Can I help you? Can I help you, sir?

GEORGIE: *(To* SERVER A*.)* Look—I asked her for two straws.

SERVER A: Excuse me, sir. Are you being served?

GEORGIE: Well, yes, but....

SERVER A: Well would you mind standing aside please? OK two big Macs with french fries, a milk-shake and a root beer coming up.

GEORGIE: Look, all I asked for was two straws. *(They carry on yelling their orders regardless.)* Can I have two straws please? *(Getting frantic.)*

SERVERS A & B: Have a nice meal! *(They freeze.)*

GEORGIE: Oh what's the use eh? It's like talking to a plastic wall in 'ere. Now where's Sharon?

(A swings round as THE HUNK *and sits on chair making eyes at* SHARON*.)*

GEORGIE: Oh rats! Look at that! Turn yer back on 'er for a moment and she's off with someone else!

*(*GEORGIE *grabs 'milkshake' and 'cheeseburger' from counter and walks to 'table' where* SHARON *and* THE HUNK *are sitting. He thumps them down on the table.)*

GEORGIE: One cheeseburger and a milkshake. Orright?!!

HUNK (A): You wouldn't happen to have another straw would you?

GEORGIE: Aaagh! *(To audience.)* Fat lot of use me havin'

136

a girl friend! She doesn't even like me. Just a stop-gap, that's what I am, till she meets the next Hunk that happens to pass by. I mean, where's the point in that, eh? Oh, what's the point in anything!!

(He storms out of the restaurant and stands with back to audience. A, B & C *become* MODELS *in shop window.* GEORGIE *strolls round and looks in the window.)*

GEORGIE: *(Reading sign.)* 'Nina's Fashions.' I mean, why bother wearing clothes, eh? Well they only make you sweat, don't they! *(Turns to window, and combs his hair. Then he sees it.)* Oh no—a dirty great zit! No wonder Sharon doesn't like me—I've got huge great boils all over me face!! *(He turns to the window and squeezes the spot—hitting one of the* MODELS *in the eye. The* MODEL *reacts accordingly.)* Oh, it's all a waste of time, isn't it? *(He wipes his fingers on his shirt.)* Well don't just stand there *(to dummies).* Is it a waste of time or isn't it, eh? I mean, what's the point of it all? Why stand there all day, waitin' for people to squeeze zits at you, eh? I mean, where's the point in that? *(He turns to window again and freezes in horror as he sees his reflection.)* Oh no! What's the point of me? What *is* the point of me? Oh, I need a walk.

(He walks to rear of stage and turns his back to the audience. B & C *become park gates,* A *is the* PARKY, *moving chairs to form park bench.* PARKY *locks one gate as* GEORGIE *walks through the other and sits on the bench.* GEORGIE *has not seen* PARKY *yet.* PARKY *goes to lock the other gate and sees* GEORGIE.)

PARKY (A): C'mon then, let's be 'avin' you.

GEORGIE: You lockin' up then?

(He walks forward and stares upwards.)

PARKY(A): 'Fraid so. This park closes at 9.30 prompt.

What you lookin' at then?

GEORGIE: Eh...oh, just the stars. There's thousands of 'em up there—all of them little worlds...

PARKY (A): Not all of 'em son. Half of them are dead.

GEORGIE: Eh?

PARKY (A): Y'see, it takes ages for the light to get from there to 'ere. So you're lookin' at what the universe looked like years ago. Meantime, alf of them have exploded. Called 'Novas' they are—I read up on stars once.

GEORGIE: Y'mean—half of them are dead, and there's no way of tellin'?

PARKY(A): Not with the naked eye, mate. Yer need a telescope for that.

(PARKY goes to rear of stage with back to audience.)

GEORGIE: What's the point of a universe that's half dead, eh? And anyhow how come huge great stars like that can disappear and nobody notices? And what about me...I could die and nobody would even notice!

(A, B & C become SALVATION ARMY BAND, marching up and down 'playing' 'Onward Christian Soldiers'. One member uses chair as euphonium.)

GEORGIE: Eh? What's goin' on here. *(Then marches along with band mocking them.)* The Sally Army: they're out every Friday, regular as closin' time! *(To band.)* 'Ello—working late aren't we?

CAPTAIN (A): *(Standing on chair.)* Now our songster leader is going to read from the Scriptures. Thank you, Margaret.

MARGARET (C): The Parable of the Lost Son. Jesus went on to say there was once a man who had two sons. The younger one said to his father, 'Father, give me my share of the property now.' So the man divided

138

his property between his two sons and....

GEORGIE: Anyhow, to cut a long story short, right, it turns out this kid clears off with the readies and has a good time—you know worr I mean? When he's spent up, the country's hit by a recession and he has to try to get a job. All he can get is a YTS scheme, training to be a pig breeder. That means he gets to feed 'em. And he's so hungry, right, he wants to eat the swill what they give the pigs. And he thinks: 'Blow this for a lark—I'll go home and work for me old man: at least then I'll get fed proper.' So he ups and goes 'ome. And when he gets there, his old man's waitin' to greet him with open arms! He says he's sorry, right, but his dad's so pleased to see him, he says it'll be just like before, and throws a big party.

Nice story, eh? Next thing, this old boy—the Sally Army bloke—gets up to speak. He says, right, that this story is all about me, that I'm lost and what I need to do is to say sorry to God. Who? That's what I said. Turns out this God made me and everything else (even them stars what have gone out), and that everyone's run away from him to have it easy, like. But God, he's just waitin' for us to get back to him and say sorry. Then—according to this bloke—*you'll* find out what's the point of life. All I've got to do is say sorry to God and ask him to have me back....

So I did! I stood there on the corner of our street and said, 'God—if you're there, I'm 'ere!' Stupid really, 'cos I'm 'ere whether he is or not if you see what I mean.... But, anyway, I says I'm sorry and if he's willin' to have me, I'm ready to come back. I didn't feel very different, like, yer know, no shots up the arm, or green hairs growin' out of me or anythin', but then they told me that's what it's like anyway. Then I went home.

Me mum and dad came rushin' out to greet me....

(A & B *become* MUM *and* DAD, *running in slow motion across stage towards* GEORGIE.)

MUM: Georgie, Georgie, you're home! I'm so glad. I have been waiting up for you. I've made you some supper: sausage sandwiches, your favourite!

DAD: 'Ello son: I've been down the labour and I've got you a job testing sports cars down at Brands Hatch. Can you start on Monday?

GEORGIE: Then we went in, and we had this fantastic party—with all me mates n' that—and I got off with Sharon's big sister, Cheryl!

GEORGIE *goes to kiss* C (*as* CHERYL) *who is standing on a chair and is therefore much taller. They are interrupted by* A *coughing loudly.*)

GEORGIE: (*Sheepishly.*) Actually, er, it didn't really happen like that. It was more like this really....

(*The scene is now played again, as it really happened*—MUM *and* DAD *seated in front of telly.*)

MUM: (*Standing.*) What time do yer call this then?!

GEORGIE: I dunno—what time do you make it?

MUM: It's gone eleven! You should have been 'ere by half-past ten!

GEORGIE: Why, what happened then?

(MUM *moves towards him with violence in her eyes!*)

GEORGIE: I was only round the corner....

MUM: You could have been in Timbuctoo for all we knew—yer father's been worried sick, 'aven't yer Fred. Fred! Listen when I'm tellin' him will yer.

DAD: (*Who has not moved.*) Eh...?

MUM: I dunno, I bend over backwards for you kids, but wassapoint, eh?

GEORGIE: Funny you should mention 'wassapoint' Mum, 'cos I've been thinkin' tonight, and I reckon that....

MUM: Yeah, well yer can think upstairs in bed now then. Go on, or you'll be moanin' in the mornin' when you have to get up!

GEORGIE: All right, I'm goin'....

(He walks to a chair and stands on it i.e. he goes upstairs. TV turns MUM and DAD off again.)

GEORGIE: Y'see, it's not that easy, even when you have found out wossapoint. (Reaches up for light-cord.)

Tararabit. *(Pulls light-cord and as it 'clicks', he freezes.)*

Ruby's Story

Although written after 'Georgie', 'Ruby's Story' is a lot more conventional in that real entrances and exits are used, with the scenes more separate and distinct. Nonetheless, some scenes do run into one another and, again, there's a lot of doubling-up to do. In addition to this, good use is made of a chanted rhyme, to the tune of 'Paddy from Home' (if that helps). This changes slightly to give a recurring 'up-date' on the story. Also, the more abstract device of a 'chorus' is used to add sounds and rhythm to the different scenes.

In all then, 'Ruby' is a bit more stagey than 'Georgie' —and gives everyone a chance to flex their vocal chords, which adds a bit of variety.

As for the plot—corny isn't the word! A real 'rags to riches' (and back to rags) story. So make the most of the fact and enjoy it!

Main characters: RUBY
MAX
HARRY IRVINE

Incidental characters: CHORUS
ANGIE
HEADMASTER
JOHN
SMITH and DOCHERTY (in Job
Centre)
MISS SHELLEY WINTHROP
COMPERE
REPORTERS
SECRETARY
GOSSIPS

In our production, the characters are divided out like this:

Hazel—Ruby
Sue   —Angie, and all parts marked as 'A'
Fraser—Harry Irvine and all parts marked as
'B'
Ray   —Max and all parts marked as 'C'

The chorus consists of A, B and C.

Costume: Basic performing strip, plus jacket and
flat cap for Max.

Props: Three small chairs (as per 'Georgie')
Sandwich Boards with front inscription:
"FEAR NOT, FOR I HAVE REDEEMED
YOU" and back inscription: "I HAVE

CALLED YOU BY NAME"
Broom
Dummy Microphone

School Assembly
(*RUBY, ANGIE (A) and JOHN (C), stand in a line across the stage, with their backs to the audience.* HEADMASTER (B) *stands front stage left, frozen in position. With backs still to audience,* ANGIE, JOHN *and* RUBY *begin singing....*)

Ruby will be all the rage
When she struts upon the stage.
To see her name upon the page,
That is all she lives for.

ANGIE (A) & JOHN (C): (*Chanting as they turn.*) Ru-bee (*clap x 3*), Ru-bee (*clap x 3*), Ru-bee (*clap x 3*).

RUBY: (*Turning.*) Hi everybody, thanks for coming.

ANGIE (A): Sssh Ruby, he'll hear yer!

RUBY: Eh? Oh sorry....

HEADMASTER (B): You're all going out into a big world. An exciting world, a world full of promise, of opportunity....

ANGIE (A): Honestly, Ruby, you don't half ask for trouble.

RUBY: Sorry—I was just thinkin'...

HEADMASTER (B): ...And I know, I just *know* you won't disappoint me. You'll go out there and *do* something with your lives. And remember—once a Greenmonk boy or girl, *always* a Greenmonk boy or girl.

RUBY: Streuth, don't he go on.

HEADMASTER (B): ...As our founder once said...

RUBY: 'Ere, what you doin' when yer finish, John?

JOHN (C): Eh? Oh, dunno—sign on I suppose....

RUBY: What? I thought your dad was gettin' you a job.

JOHN (C): He was. But he got made redundant.

145

HEADMASTER (B): ...So, finally, boys and girls of the Fifth form...

RUBY: How about you, Angie?

ANGIE (A): Well, er, actually, I think...well that is....

RUBY: Yer goin' to be a missionary, right?!

ANGIE (A): *(Defensively.)* Did I say that?

RUBY: No....

ANGIE (A): Yeah, you're right. I fink, like, God's callin' me to do it, so I will. *(Embarrassed pause—*JOHN *sniggers.)* How about you, Rube?

JOHN (C): God's callin' 'er to be rich and famous!!

RUBY: Shut up you!

(ANGIE *digs her in the ribs.)*

HEADMASTER (B): ...And finally....

RUBY: *(Keeping her voice down.)* I do want to be rich and famous, but I don't need anyone tellin' me to!

HEADMASTER (B): ...Well, I can say no more than this....

JOHN (C): I've heard that before.

HEADMASTER (B): ...And good luck. *(They pick up their bags to go.)*...And remember....

JOHN (C): See what I mean?

ANGIE (A): You serious, Rube, about bein' a dancer 'n' that?

RUBY: Yeah, 'course I am.

HEADMASTER (B): Dismissed.

JOHN (C): Well how you gonna get a job then?

RUBY: Job Centre, stupid.

(They leave the 'hall' and the scene changes to Job Centre. SMITH *is seated, with* DOCHERTY—*a 'heavy' —in the background. A exits.)*

SMITH (B): Next!

(Enter RUBY, *for an interview. She sits in the vacant seat.)*

RUBY: Good mornin'.

SMITH (B): Is it?

RUBY: Eh? I dunno.

SMITH (B): Mmm—indecisive; that won't help you. Will Miss...er...(*looks at form*)...Cube, what is it this time? Prime Minister is it? Chairperson of ICI, eh? I'm afraid we're right out of 'wife to the heir of the throne' jobs! Still, I'm sure we can think of something. Well, what do you fancy?

RUBY: I want to be famous.

SMITH (B): Oh I see—feminist tack, eh? First female steeplejack, that sort of thing?

RUBY: No. I want to be a dancer, and a singer.

SMITH (B): A dancer and a singer, eh? Well Ruby— Ruby *Cube*! Ha, ha, well I'm sure we'll be able to *solve* this one, eh, Docherty: Ruby Cube—solve this one! (SMITH *laughs hysterically*. DOCHERTY *laughs stupidly*.)

RUBY: Yeah, very funny. I'd like to carry on livin' at home at first, so if you can find me somethin' local....

SMITH (B): Good grief—you're serious! Docherty, she's serious. She actually wants to be a dancer!!

DOCHERTY (C): Well—tell her to run away to the circus then! (*They laugh again.*)

RUBY: Look, just give me the details and I'll fix up an interview for the job meself.

(SMITH *and* DOCHERTY *collect themselves.*)

SMITH (B): Miss Cube.....

DOCHERTY (C): Ruby....

SMITH (B): They just don't exist.

RUBY: What, jobs?!

SMITH (B): Generally, no. But especially, *especially* Ruby, jobs for dancers.

DOCHERTY (C): Unless of course, you're a dancer....

SMITH (B): In which case they're very hard to come by.

DOCHERTY (C): And as for singers, Ruby....

SMITH (B): Singers are two-a-penny, Ruby. Sorry.

RUBY: But I can dance, a bit. And sing.

SMITH (B): Nothing, sorry.

(RUBY *gets up to go, and is pulled back down by* SMITH.)

SMITH (B): Now, if you was to want to be a famous hair stylist....

DOCHERTY (C): If you was to be *sharp* with the old scissors.

SMITH (B): They're just cryin' out for young *blades* like yourself.

DOCHERTY (C): A *cut* above the dole queue, Ruby.

SMITH (B): Keep you in *trim* 'n' all, eh Docherty? Ha ha.

DOCHERTY (C): Oh yeah—just the job for a *curl* like you!

(*They collapse in laughter again, and after some moments collect themselves.*)

SMITH (B): Well, Miss Cube?

DOCHERTY (C): There's plenty more out there, just *dyin'* for a chance like this, Ruby.

SMITH (B): About four-and-a-half million more, to be precise.

RUBY: You mean—there's nothin' at all for dancers...?

SMITH (B): Nothin', Ruby. Sorry.

RUBY: OK I'll try for that, then. It'll be a start.

SMITH (B): (*Handing over an address card.*) *Hair* you are then, Miss Cube....

DOCHERTY (C): (*Taking it from* SMITH *and giving it to a confused* RUBY.) ...Sharon's Poodle Parlour, 3.30 p.m.

SMITH (B): Next!

(RUBY *starts to leave, then, turning round, slaps*

148

SMITH *across the face and exits.* DOCHERTY *laughs stupidly at* SMITH, *until* SMITH *thumps him in the stomach. They freeze at the point of impact. Freeze is held for a few seconds, then* A *enters and the scene changes to a hair dressing salon.* A, B & C *stand in a line, each with a chair in front of them. They make stylized cutting/combing movements to the chant as* RUBY *enters.)*

CHORUS: Sweep, snip, tints, rinse,
Sweep, snip, tints, rinse,
Sweep, snip, tints,
Sweep, snip, tints,
Sweep, snip,
Sweep, snip,
Sweep, sweep, sweep, sweep, sweep
(etc. continues quietly in background).

RUBY: *(Sweeping.)* Huh, some chance of stardom 'ere. Three months' slog and the only cut they've let me have is in me wages! Ain't no one goin' to know me from Adam if I work 'ere all me life. Flamin' slave labour, it is. If only...if only I could get a break, I just know I could do it, then everybody'd know me. I'd be really famous.... *(Then, breaking into song....)*
Fame! I'm gonna live for ever,
Light up the sky with my name—Fame!

CHORUS: *(Cutting her off and moving into dramatic poses.)*
A: Snip!
B: Tints!
C: Rinse!
*(*RUBY *sees a newspaper on the floor. She picks it up.)*

RUBY: 'Ere...*(reading).*

CHORUS: *(Relaxing poses, resuming movements.)* Snip, tints, rinse *(etc.)*

RUBY: Wow!

CHORUS: Ruby will be all the rage
       When she struts upon the stage.
       To see her name upon the page,
       Is all she ever lives for.
   (Exit C.)

RUBY: This is it! A talent contest. The Spanner 'n' Works, 8 p.m. Saturday. Right, that does it! I'll show 'em.
   (Exit RUBY. Chairs are placed in a row, stage right, by A & B, who then become grinning contestants. Enter C, as MAX, with microphone.)

MAX: And finally tonight, we have the very lovely Miss Ruby Cube. Hello Ruby, my love. That's it, just stand there. Great. Now tell me, Ruby—actually that's a very unusual name, isn't it?—Ruby Cube.

RUBY: Well, it was me mum and dad's idea—'course, they weren't around then, Max.

MAX: Who—yer Mum 'n' Dad?

RUBY: No—the cubes, yer know....

MAX: Oh, I see *(he doesn't)*. Ha, ha...well anyway— what are you goin' to do for us tonight, Ruby?

RUBY: I'm goin' to sing and dance, Max.

MAX: You're goin' to sing and dance, Ruby.

RUBY: Yes, that's right, Max.

MAX: And what are you goin' to sing and dance for us Ruby? *(She whispers in his ear.)* Great. And I gather the other contestants are goin' to join you, is that right Ruby?

RUBY: Yes, Max.

MAX: Isn't that great, ladies and gentlemen. Well, here she is, the very lovely Miss Ruby Cube.
   (A & B now do robotic-type dancing in the back-ground, and hum, as RUBY sings very loud, to the

tune of Toyah's "I'm gonna turn this world upside down".)

RUBY: I'm gonna turn my anorak inside out!
I'm gonna wear my glasses upside down!
I'm gonna run round the classroom,
scream and shout!
I'm gonna sit in the library and sing very loud!!
I wanna be free
I wanna be me!

(On the last note, she is chopped down by one of the rival competitors—A—who has been moving closer and closer during the dance. RUBY lies on the floor until MAX comes to her rescue and helps her up. A & B take their seats and resume their inane grinning at the audience.)

MAX: *(Casting menacing glance at A & B.)* Oh, very bad luck that for Ruby, ladies and gentlemen, but I'm sure, like me, you saw what a great little performer she is already.

Well, you've voted, and the winner is *(very disappointed)* Miss Shelley Winthrop—flippin' 'eck—for "The Good Ship Lollypop".

SHELLY W (A): *(Who pushed RUBY. To audience.)* Oh thank you, thank you. I love you all! Thank you....

(B kisses her outflung hand, and with great pomp they exit, leaving MAX and RUBY alone.)

MAX: Well that's all for tonight, ladies and gentlemen. Thank you and good night. *(To RUBY.)* Hey Ruby—I'm sorry, love. You would've won that easy if it weren't for that little trollop Winthrop.

RUBY: That's all right, Max *(sniffling)*. I guess I just wasn't good enough....

MAX: Rubbish—you wiped the floor with her! Look, yer've got to aim higher—otherwise you'll never get on. Over at The Albany, they have some real classy acts. There's an open contest once a year and it comes up this month. Get yerself a decent outfit and win the competition—a tenner should cover it. *(He pushes a tenner into her hand.)*

RUBY: Who, me?

MAX: Why not—yer good enough, aren't yer?

RUBY: I dunno....

MAX: 'Course you are—you'll walk it.

RUBY: *(She hesitates, then takes it and gives him a big hug.)* Oh, thanks, Max! *(She turns to leave.)*

MAX: Oh and er...change the name, eh?

(They freeze. The freeze is held for a few seconds, then both exit, stage left. From stage right, enter A as an up-market COMPERE.)

COMPERE (A): And, now, the moment you've all been waiting for—remember, the winner receives two thousand pounds and a recording contract with MFI records. So it's instant stardom for the lucky winner.

Ladies and gentlemen, this year's Albany Star is—Miss Ruby C.

(Enter RUBY accompanied by C, stage left. At same time, B enters, stage right. B & C make sound of applause. A, B & C walk to front stage and become REPORTERS while RUBY freezes, centre stage in pose.)

REPORTERS: *(Typing.)*

B: RUBY—A BRIGHT NEW GEM TAKES BRITAIN BY STORM.

C: HOME-LOVING MISS C WINS TALENT CONTEST.

A: WHISTLE-STOP TOUR FOR RUBY C.

C: BRITISH CHARTS SHATTERED BY RISING STAR.

B: "AMERICA HERE I COME," SAYS SUPERSTAR RUBY.

> *(They freeze, then swing round to photograph* RUBY, *who runs through several poses as they 'click' their cameras. Then* A, B & C *become TV interviewers.)*

A: Hey, Miss Ruby, what's it like to be No.1 twelve weeks running?

RUBY: Well, it's really nice, I mean really cool.

C: Is it true you're doing another TV series, Miss C?

RUBY: Yeah, that is right.

B: Which channel Miss C?

RUBY: All of 'em!

C: Hey, Miss Ruby, there's rumours that you've become a Christian. Is it true?

RUBY: Yeah, that is true.

A: How did it happen?

RUBY: A letter, from a friend.

B: And are you really getting married, Miss C?

RUBY: Look, Cliff and I are just good friends....

CHORUS: *(Singing.)*

> Ruby C is all the rage,
> See how she struts upon the stage,
> And see her name upon the page.
> It's all she's ever lived for.

> *(They freeze. Scene changes to* HARRY *Irvine's office.* HARRY *is seated, stage left, reading 'Smash Hits'.* C *exits.* A *becomes* SECRETARY.)*

SECRETARY (A): OK Miss C, Mr Irvine will see you now.

RUBY: Ta, luv. 'Ere Harry what's all this about then?

HARRY: *(Without looking up.)* Hello, Ruby, siddown. *(She does so.)* Now let's get down to business. Do you know how many records you sold last week?

RUBY: No—how many?

HARRY: Six. That's not counting your foreign sales, of course.

RUBY: Well, I 'ad a sore throat, didn't I.

HARRY: No Ruby, you had competition.

RUBY: What?!

HARRY: Look. *(He gives her the magazine and begins to pace around.)* Papers, magazines, everything's full of 'em.

RUBY: Who?! Mandy Finch and the Finchettes?! What kind of drivel's that?

HARRY: That's not drivel, Ruby. That's *money*.

RUBY: But they've all got flared trousers, and horrible nylon jumpers from Marks an' Sparks. And fluffy slippers! I don't believe it!

HARRY: You better believe it, Ruby. That's 'Square Rock', and it's big.

RUBY: But it's rubbish!

HARRY: Ruby, I know that. You know that. But do they know that?! *(He gestures towards audience.)*

RUBY: Well, it's only a craze, they'll soon get over it.

HARRY: No, Ruby, in this business, crazes are what make or break people. You either get into the craze, or go under.

RUBY: Now look. Ruby C ain't wearin' fluffly slippers for no one.

HARRY: Oh you will Ruby, or you'll never make another record.

RUBY: But Harry....

HARRY: No 'buts' Ruby. Do you know what MFI records stands for? I'll tell yer. 'Money For Irvine.' I'm losing money on you, so you'd better get over to Marks and Spencers and get yourself a new outfit.

RUBY: And if I don't?

HARRY: You'll go back to the poodle parlour.

RUBY: Not a chance—Ruby C's a household name.

HARRY: Not any more, it's not.

RUBY: We'll see about that!!

(RUBY *exits*. A, B & C *become* REPORTERS, *front stage, typing*.)

A: 'NO FLUFFY SLIPPERS FOR ME,' says Ruby C.

C: 'SQUARE ROCK IS RUBBISH,' says former Rock Star.

B: FOURTEEN WEEKS AT THE TOP FOR THE FINCHETTES AND STILL CLIMBING!!

C: 'MANDY'S SECRET' BY NEW MANAGER, HARRY IRVINE.

CHORUS: Boo, hiss, fizzle, flop,
        Boo, hiss, fizzle, flop,
        Boo, hiss, fizzle,
        Boo, hiss, fizzle,
        Boo, hiss,
        Boo, hiss,
        Boo, hiss,
        Boo, hisssssss....

(*They turn their backs on* RUBY, *who has entered, stage right, and walked to front stage*.)

RUBY: Remember me? I'm Ruby C. I can't go back to the poodle parlour....

CHORUS: (*Singing*.)
        Ruby C was all the rage,
        She used to dance upon the stage.
        Can't see her name upon the page,
        Now what's she got to live for?

RUBY: Streuth, no one even remembers me name. Even when I tell them C was short for 'Cube'.

GOSSIP (B): Oh yeah—that's a good 'un.

GOSSIP (C): What are yer—commedienne.

(They laugh, then freeze again.)

RUBY: An' the worst thing is, no one'll give you a job—not even at the Spanner 'n' Works—unless yer wear flared trousers and nylon jumpers. Not to mention fluffy slippers. Even me Mum and Dad call me Mandy. Used to be such a laugh, now no one even remembers me name.

GOSSIP (A): Poor love. Still, makes a change from 'Napolean', dunnit! *(Exits.)*

GOSSIP (C): Ruby who? Now don't tell me—the face is familiar, but I can't quite remember the name.... *(Exits.)*

GOSSIP (B): 'Ere, didn't she used to be on *Coronation Street*...? *(Exit, stage left.)*

RUBY: Get lost, yer silly old bag!!

(As B has made his exit, MAX has entered, stage right, wearing sandwich board and cap. He assumes that RUBY was talking to him.)

MAX: Oh all right then—I didn't mean to upset yer....

RUBY: What?

MAX: *(Turning to go.)* No, No, it's all right, don't matter....

RUBY: Max! Max! Max!!! Oh Max!!!

MAX: *(Nods.)* Ruby.

RUBY: Oh Max!!! *(To audience.)* It was Max.

MAX: I've been lookin' for you all over. You owe me a tenner.

RUBY: Oh Max!

(She flings her arms around him. Then notices the sandwich board.)

RUBY: Max, what on earth have you got on?

MAX: Eh? Oh this. It's me new job: sandwichboard man. It says....

RUBY: I can read, Max.

MAX: Aye, but it's yer audience yer've got to think about. *(He starts reading to the audience.)* It says, 'Fear not, for I have redeemed you....' That means he's bought yer back.... *(He freezes.)*

RUBY: *(To audience.)* Turns out old Max got to be a Christian 'cos he seen me on the telly when I was tellin' everyone about how good it was. You see, Angela had written to me nearly every week while I was busy livin' it up—tellin' me that God loved me and that he wanted me to love him back....

MAX: *(To audience.)* Now, have yer got that? All right we'll start again, and this time I'll not go so fast as I can see yer a bit slow.... *(He freezes.)*

RUBY: Thing is, I forgot all about Jesus when things got bad. Or maybe things got bad when I forgot about Jesus.... Anyway, what I forgot and what Max told me, was that God promised he'd never forget me even when I forgot him. *(She's getting a bit confused.)* Like the verse.

MAX: OK. Second Part. *(He turns round, with his back to audience.)* 'I have called you by name,' *(To* RUBY.) Ruby Cube.

RUBY: Oh, Max—you remembered.

MAX: 'Course I did *(to audience).* Two people never forget. One's elephant—that's me, and the other's God.

RUBY: And, now, well I mean it's tough not being a star no more, but, well, now I can face it, 'cos I know me name'll always be remembered by someone, even if everyone else forgets it.

MAX: *(Looking at his watch.)* Hey—c'mon. We're runnin' over. Let's go and 'ave a cuppa tea.

RUBY: Hang on—we've got to finish.

RUBY & MAX: *(Singing.)*

Ruby Cube has left the stage,
Her name is never on the page,
But she will never be the same,
She's everything to live for.

MAX: *(Putting on his cap.)* Right. That's that then. *(He links arms with* RUBY *and turns away from audience.)* You know, I really think they're beginning to catch on.

(They freeze, looking back over their shoulders as if at a camera.)

THE END

More to Read

Theory

John McGrath, *A Good Night Out (Popular Theatre: Audience Class and Form)* (Methuen)

Preparation and rehearsal

Steve & Janet Stickley and Jim Bellen, *Using the Bible in Drama* (Bible Society)
Clive Barker, *Theatre Games* (Eyre Methuen)
Geoffrey & Judith Stevenson, *Steps of Faith (A Practical Introduction to Mime and Dance)* (Kingsway

Publications)
John Hodgson & Ernest Richards, *Improvisation* (Eyre
  Methuen)

Scripts

Steve & Janet Stickley and Jim Bellen, *Using the Bible
  in Drama* (Bible Society)
Paul Burbridge & Murray Watts, *Time to Act* (Hodder
  & Stoughton)
Paul Burbridge & Murray Watts, *Lightning Sketches*
  (Hodder & Stoughton)

Advanced Training

C. Stanislavski, *An Actor Prepares* (Eyre Methuen)
Cicely Berry, *The Voice and the Actor* (Harrap)